GRIMSBY TOWN

THROUGH THE TRAP DOOR
THE ROAD TO HELL 2001-2010

DESERT ISLAND BOOKS 'THROUGH THE TRAP DOOR' SERIES

	ISBN
WREXHAM: THROUGH THE TRAP DOOR 1998-2008	978-1-905328-49-9
LUTON: THROUGH THE TRAP DOOR 2004-2009	978-1-905328-66-6
GRIMSBY: THROUGH THE TRAP DOOR 2001-2010	978-1-905328-81-9

GRIMSBY TOWN

Through the Trap Door
THE ROAD TO HELL 2001-2010

Series editor: Clive Leatherdale

Rob Hadgraft

DESERT ISLAND BOOKS

First published in 2010
by
DESERT ISLAND BOOKS LIMITED
7 Clarence Road, Southend on Sea, Essex SS1 1AN
United Kingdom
www.desertislandbooks.com

British Library Cataloguing-in-Publication Data
A catalogue record for this book is available from the British Library

ISBN 978-1-905328-81-9

Printed in Great Britain

The author and publishers gratefully acknowledge
Michael White and Grimsby Town FC for kind permission
to reproduce photographs in this book

Contents

Author's Note

I'm one of those people who loves a good coincidence. And I reckon Grimsby Town's sad exit from the Football League in the spring of 2010 has thrown up a number of corkers. For one thing, it occurred exactly 100 years – almost to the day – after the only other occasion such a calamity befell this famous old club.

The Mariners' first demotion came after a win-or-bust clash with Gainsborough Trinity on the final day of the 1909-10 season. The game ended all square, which meant Grimsby finished one place and one point behind their opponents. It meant Grimsby had to go cap in hand to the Football League's AGM at the Imperial Hotel in London, hoping to secure enough re-election votes to survive.

Shockingly, delegates from the other clubs turned their backs on Grimsby and only a meagre dozen votes were mustered. The eager young tykes of Huddersfield Town (beaten twice only recently by Grimsby's Reserves) polled more than twice as many votes (26) and the Mariners were banished after eighteen years' League membership. They dropped miserably into the Midland League to play alongside the likes of Denaby, Mexborough and Worksop.

But Grimbarians are nothing if not resilient and once everybody at Blundell Park had got over the shock, club captain 'Chopper' Lee rallied his men. He urged them to work for an instant return to the League – and this was duly achieved twelve months later when the Midland League title was won by a single point from Sheffield Wednesday Reserves.

One hundred years later, the club finds itself needing another leader in the mould of Chopper Lee, in order to repeat the trick. Perhaps it's an omen, then, that the modern-day team captain is also called Lee (Lee Peacock, to be precise). The two captains' shared name is by no means the only other coincidence in this story either, for that disastrous 1909-10 season was remarkably similar to the one which ended 100 years later with the same grisly outcome:

For example, in 1909-10 Grimsby started badly and won just three of their first 26 league matches; in 2009-10 they also managed just three wins from the first 26 games. Also, Chopper Lee's men were chased out of the FA Cup in an embarrassing defeat by a west country non-league side (Bristol Rovers); 100 years later Grimsby were also knocked out of the competition by a west country non-league side (Bath City).

And what's more, by the end of the 1909-10 season Grimsby had won just nine games in total, meaning they finished second from bottom of the entire League; 100 years later they also won a total of just nine games in 2009-10, and also finished second from bottom.

Now is that spooky, or what?

Many will say they saw the 2010 demotion coming a year or two earlier, but it was nevertheless a major shock to the system for a club with such a long history and traditions. The Mariners are one of England's oldest senior clubs, having been formed 132 years previously. They were founder members of Division Two, and it's often forgotten that they have enjoyed three separate spells in football's top flight, the last of which ended with a club record 0-8 defeat at Arsenal as recently as 1948. Indeed, the club enjoyed uninterrupted Football League status for 99 years before the dreaded trap door swung open in May 2010.

Now the club has to regroup and face life in the Blue Square Conference, following two very difficult years of struggle at, or near, the bottom of the League's basement division.

This book – part of a series of Desert Island Football Histories covering clubs which fell through the trap door (following Wrexham in 2008 and Luton Town a year later) – charts the decline that led to this calamity. It was a decline that effectively can be traced to Blundell Park during 2001, immediately after Town enjoyed a very brief spell at the top of the second tier. From the summit they began an alarming slide downwards during that autumn, and were given a hefty push on their way thanks to the financial implications of the ITV Digital collapse. With only a few brief interruptions, it has been pretty much downhill ever since.

Automatic promotion and relegation between the League and Conference was introduced in 1987, since when precious few clubs have been able to bounce back immediately after tumbling through the trap door (neighbours Lincoln City were one, back in 1988). But plenty of others have made it back eventually. Probably the most encouraging statistic for Grimsby fans is that more than 50 per cent of all the demoted clubs have at some point managed to return to the League.

Of the 25 who vanished through the trap door since 1987 (not including Grimsby), fourteen have engineered a return. Rising like a Phoenix from the ashes have come Torquay, Exeter, Shrewsbury, Doncaster, Colchester, Lincoln, Hereford, Aldershot, Barnet, Carlisle, Oxford, Darlington, Halifax and Chester. The last three on the list actually suffered demotion twice. For the 2010-11 season, Grimsby find themselves alongside Luton, Darlington, Kidderminster, Rushden & Diamonds, Cambridge United, Wrexham, York and Mansfield as Conference clubs intent on making a return to former League glories. Southport and Newport County are also there – two clubs who exited the Football League prior to 1987.

To complete the picture, we should spare a thought for the six former League clubs whose troubles went from bad to worse after demotion, and which ended up sliding even lower than the Conference Premier, or folding altogether. These were Halifax, Maidstone, Boston, Newport County, Scarborough and Chester.

On a more positive note, two clubs have not only returned from the wilderness, but have gone on to achieve unprecedented success. Doncaster Rovers dropped in 1998, scandal-ridden, penniless and with a ramshackle ground, and looking like they'd never be seen again. Twelve years later they occupy a place in the Championship and enjoy a reputation as one of the best footballing sides outside the Premiership. Colchester United, meanwhile, went down in 1990 but returned two years later, going on to reach Championship level in 2006 for the first time in their history. These two proved emphatically that there is life after the Conference.

At Blundell Park, much will depend on how quickly Grimsby can find their feet in the new surroundings under Neil Woods' leadership. A win at big-spending Crawley Town on the opening day of 2010-11 season was a fine start. But whatever their fate in the nerve-racking subsequent months, you get the feeling they won't be away from the 92 Club for very long.

In putting this book together I've been struck by the passion, stoicism and humour of Town's die-hard fans, as evidenced by the excellent websites *Cod Almighty* and *The Fishy (the Electronic Fishcake)*. These were useful research sources, along with the *Grimsby Telegraph*, and not forgetting Dave Wherry's updated tome *The Grimsby Town Story* (Yore, 2008). I would also like to gratefully acknowledge the help of Austin Mitchell MP, who wrote the Foreword to this book, and the backroom staff at Blundell Park, particularly Lucie Ramsden. All action pictures are reproduced with kind permission of photographer Michael White and Grimsby Town FC. Thanks also to fellow writers Spencer Austin and Pete Green.

ROB HADGRAFT
September 2010

Foreword

by Austin Mitchell MP

I'm not going to claim to be a great football fan. Nor am I the best atten-
der at Blundell Park. Yet I am a Grimsby Town enthusiast and I've
watched the snakes and ladders career of the Mariners over the three and
a half decades I've been Borough Member with enormous interest and
intermittent despair. The up and down switchback of their performances and the recent cliff-hanging tension, all so well chronicled by Rob
Hadgraft, have been a bit of a strain on ageing hearts and arteries. Mine
and everyone else's.

It's good to have Town's tale so well retold, and to savour again the
highs, the lows, the excitement and the tensions, with the personalities
and the problems off the field all brought out so well.

This isn't quite on the scale of Tolstoy's *War and Peace*, but is important for us in our little corner of the world and for the Diaspora of
Grimbarians spread all round the world (I've bumped into them in New
Caledonia, Papua New Guinea and Tokyo, and all asked me about the
Mariners). When Grimsby fell out of the League the whole town held its
breath, calculated and recalculated the points, hoped against hope, before
falling into depression.

Grimsby Town is important to Grimsby. We walk a little taller when it
does well. We're depressed by the fall and baffled on the occasions when
they've gone on for so long without winning, despite the best advice we
offer so liberally from the sidelines.

Rob tells the tale in terms of the games, the players and the personalities. As a politician I see it in terms of what the story says about our
town. The football team is rooted in the community and its fortunes
reflect the changes in the town and in the lives of a community which is
a bit more remote and still a bit special. Right at the start in 1878 when a
group of cricketers got together to give themselves something to do in
the winter, Town, then called Grimsby Pelham, in deference to the local
aristocracy whose rotten borough Grimsby had been, was part of the
movement to civic improvement and to growing leisure opportunities for
the people which was beginning all over the country.

When I arrived in Grimsby, Skipper Evans was one of the directors
and the great treat was the packets of fish given to the visiting teams, the
piles of prawns in the directors' room (which was unisex – mere women

were shoved into a tiny box-room next door with no prawns), and in the chants which told uppety visitors what we'd done with their fish.

Sadly, since then football has become a game of stars, and big money to buy star players and finance star facilities, and Grimsby, with fishing declining, its community smaller and less prosperous, just wasn't able to compete. The problem was compounded by the collapse of ITV Digital (which almost broke ITV too). In the increasing focus on money, excitement and the glamour-panted Premier League, we were the also-rans.

Town has had some great successes in the first decade of this century: their work with young people, the information technology training at the ground and in schools, their memorable games at Wembley and Cardiff, the strong support they've enjoyed from the *Telegraph*, the council, the town, the Institute and indeed from local MPs putting Town's case to the Inland Revenue. Yet they've also faced a long downhill slide and the personal rows and ructions, the frequent team and managerial changes, the disappointments (and mysteries) of Alan Buckley's returns and departures, all so well chronicled in Rob's book, have all been due to tightening economic difficulties.

Success and failure have become increasingly a question of money. We should all be enormously grateful for the financial support Town has had, but financing any football club is like throwing money into a bottomless pit. The Mariners have had great help from Ron Ramsden and even more generously from John Fenty, who has poured a small fortune into it. But Grimsby hasn't got the local wealth of bigger, more prosperous cities, and a team languishing down the league attracts less outside money and smaller gates. It finds star players more reluctant to come or stay.

This compounding decline can only be stopped by a fairer distribution of wealth between the top clubs and those lower down which ultimately support them. Pyramids collapse without a base. If government, the FA and the television companies don't act to ensure fairer equalisation, the future is dim for smaller towns like Grimsby. Witness the large number of similar clubs: Halifax, Oxford, Rotherham, Stockport, Chesterfield, Boston and Scarborough which have all run into difficulties. We're killing football at the roots, unless teams live in bigger and richer communities where lucrative entertainment and shopping centres can pay for them.

Take the contrast between Grimsby and Hull, which is always billed as our great rival, though in fact Town and City haven't played each other much, so opportunities to hear them sing about what Tigers do to Fish have been mercifully few. I've always been pretty condescending to Hull because our team has usually been ahead. In 2000 Hull almost went bust.

Since then, however, they've had the local good luck we lacked. Hull is bigger and richer. City has been boosted by more money and by its super new stadium from Kingston Communications, where Grimsby has only managed interior decoration (which, incidentally, baffled me because when local journalist Charlie Ekberg invited me to his book launch at 'The Talk of the Town', I rolled up at a posh hotel in London and got a lot of condescending sneers. I hadn't realised that Town's restaurant, now McMenemy's, had been dragged up-market and renamed). Town couldn't raise the money for the move to Great Coates to a bigger ground financed by shops and bigger corporate sponsorship facilities, though to be honest I'm happy with Blundell Park. It's a good, old-fashioned, cosy ground and quite big enough for our turnout, and you've got the added bonus in the Findus Stand of watching the shipping if the game gets too boring.

At the end of the day (as we politicians say), Grimsby, like too many other clubs, is in danger of being locked in a spiral of decline: less money means worse teams, means lower gates, increasing inability to attract or retain stars, and results in diminishing interest. This is happening in too many towns. It's destroying the roots of football and damaging the communities affected. It hurts the long-term prospects of a game which is going to become increasingly dependent on buying in foreign stars rather than breeding its footballers in their communities. Public attention and interest are going to be focused on the pampered, over-paid and over-exposed big stars and clubs which are being bought and sold like gold mines, and not on the deserving many, struggling to raise the money to survive, like Grimsby.

Grimsby is, thank heavens, spending money on young players and youth development but there has to be a fairer redistribution of the money in football to avoid a tragedy for football and a disaster for Grimsby. Our team, like our town, is tough and resilient. They'll fight back. We all hope they'll come back. But it's tough for Grimsby to do it on its own. There has to be a reform of football finance and a fairer distribution of the money that now dominates the game, otherwise no one will be able to write such an interesting chronicle as Rob Hadgraft has about a small-town football club.

A lot of money is coming into football, but it's wrong so much of it should go to glamour-panted premier-leaguers. We need more of it in Grimsby.

Up the Mariners!

AUSTIN MITCHELL MP

Introduction

THE BACKGROUND TO A DRAMATIC SLUMP

Rewind to the long, hot summer of 1878. Heading down to Clee Park in Grimsby to meet his cricket-loving pals is a young schoolmaster named Charlie Horn. He attracts a number of strange looks as he passes, for Charlie is clutching carefully under his arm what his friends could only describe as 'a large bag of wind'.

Before the serious business of playing cricket for Worsley CC got underway that day, Charlie and his friends kicked this 'bag of wind' around the field for a while and found they were having enormous fun. Football was still in its infancy at the time – the formation of the Football League was still ten years away – but the game was catching on fast throughout Victorian Britain. Exhilarated by their impromptu kickabout, the cricketers of Worsley reckoned good old Charlie had definitely hit on something with his makeshift bag of wind. They began talking about forming their own football team. It would be something to keep them occupied during the long winter months while they waited for the cricket season to come around again. Something to get them out of the house.

And thus, Grimsby Town FC was born. The formalities were carried out upstairs in the Wellington Arms in Freeman Street, the cricketers making their plans on a wave of optimism and enthusiasm, not to mention foaming jugs of ale. In deference to their patron, the Earl of Yareborough (family name Pelham), they initially called their team Grimsby Pelham. Within a year they'd beaten two of the leading local sides, thus convincing themselves they were now the best in town and therefore deserving of a name-change to the grander-sounding Grimsby Town FC.

Before long the new club had moved away from Clee Park to spend a few years based at Abbey Park in the middle of Grimsby, before finally settling in 1898 on the site that remains their home 112 years later. It was a piece of land available for rent and situated between the busy fish docks and the seafront attractions of the fast-growing resort of Cleethorpes. They named it Blundell Park, after nearby Blundell Avenue, and quickly erected stands and laid a playing surface.

The original blue-and-white hooped kit was upgraded to chocolate-and-blue halved shirts with white knickers, and thus suitably attired, they embarked on a programme of league football for the first time in the newly formed Combination, to add to their FA Cup adventures. Before long the club tentatively applied to join the Football League, but were rebuffed and instead joined the Football Alliance. After becoming a limited company in 1890, two years later the Football League expanded to two divisions and welcomed Grimsby with open arms. The first encounter was a 2-1 victory over Northwich Victoria. Along with Hull City, Grimsby were granted special permission to play on Sundays due to the demands of the local fish trade.

Life in Division Two was interrupted by a couple of seasons up in the top flight, and one down in the Midland League, followed by the rude intervention of the Great War of 1914-18. Relegation to the new Third Division North followed in 1920, but by 1929 Grimsby had changed the club colours to black and white stripes and had risen all the way back to Division One. Eight of the next ten years were spent in the top flight (a best finish of fifth in 1935), and the club reached two FA Cup semi-finals too, losing 0-1 to Arsenal in 1936 and to Wolves at Old Trafford in 1939. Minus an injured goalkeeper, Grimsby lost the latter semi 0-5 in front of 76,962, which is still an Old Trafford ground record in 2010.

The Mariners remained in the top flight after war again broke out in 1939, but once hostilities ceased and league football resumed, Grimsby's fortunes took a turn for the worse and relegation from Division One followed in 1948. The next twenty years were largely uneventful, spent bobbing between Second and Third Divisions, with the only real highlights being the mid-1960s cup runs and Matt Tees' prodigious goal output. Skippered at that time by future England boss Graham Taylor, Grimsby lost the services of popular manager Jimmy McGuigan in 1967 and recruited Don McEvoy of Barrow to replace him. Under the new man, the Mariners slumped to the bottom of Division Three and within a few months McEvoy, too, was gone. Local man Bill Harvey, a former Luton manager, was called in to save the sinking ship, but, agonisingly, they were relegated on the final day of the 1967-68 season by just 0.08 of a goal, the tiniest of goal-average margins.

It meant Fourth Division football for the first time at Blundell Park and the slump continued, with re-election needed a year later following a 91st placed finish, with only hapless Bradford Park Avenue below them. The lowest ever attendance for a League match at Blundell Park (1,833) had assembled for a 0-2 defeat by Brentford in the penultimate game of that season.

Just three years later the picture had changed dramatically. More than 22,000 crammed into the ground to roar the Mariners to the Fourth Division title. Just a point was needed against Exeter, but Town won 3-0.

Chief architect of the turnaround in fortunes was Lawrie McMenemy, a former Coldstream guardsman who never played senior football, but had guided Doncaster Rovers to the 1969 Fourth Division title in his first season as a manager. Now he'd emulated the feat in his opening stint at Blundell Park. He was clearly destined for bigger things and joined Southampton in 1973 to be succeeded at Grimsby by Ron Ashman.

Under Ashman, Tom Casey and then Johnny Newman, Town remained in Division Three – on one occasion even tempting US secretary of state Henry Kissinger to come along and join the 4,000 watching a 2-1 win over Gillingham. Relegation to the League basement followed in 1977, but the good times soon returned. George Kerr was the manager who restored Second Division status when Grimsby were promoted as champions during a marvellous 1979-80 campaign that also featured thrilling cup action. The brand new Findus Stand went up in 1980 and in the early to mid-1980s the club consolidated at this level, including finishes of fifth and seventh, with Dave Booth and Mick Lyons having stints in the manager's chair.

The late 1980s saw another decline set in with two successive relegations and a financial crisis, and the departure of managers Lyons and his replacement Bobby Roberts. The pattern of decline, followed by revival, was maintained by new manger Alan Buckley, who led the Mariners to two successive promotions by 1991 and a stint of some six years in the second tier of English football. Buckley left in 1994 to try his luck at West Bromwich Albion, and Brian Laws was next in the hot seat. Like his predecessor, Laws would go on to manage bigger clubs, with his period at Grimsby remembered mainly for the bizarre incident at Luton when he allegedly threw a plate of sandwiches at star forward Ivano Bonetti in the changing rooms, breaking the Italian's cheekbone and precipitating this popular player's departure.

In 1997 relegation to Division Three followed, despite a brave late rally under short-term manager Kenny Swain, and Alan Buckley returned from The Hawthorns for a second stint as manager. Buckley immediately engineered a strong promotion challenge, good runs in both the major cups, plus a place in the final of the Football League Trophy, the club's first visit to Wembley Stadium. Goals from Kingsley Black and Wayne Burnett in extra-time beat AFC Bournemouth, and within five weeks of lifting the trophy the Mariners were back on the hallowed turf to face Northampton in the Division Two play-off final. This time Kevin Donovan bagged a first-half winner to spark celebrations in front of the 20,000 travelling 'cod-heads'. Crowds of more than 62,000 attended both Grimsby games under the twin towers.

That glorious spring of 1998 is still fondly remembered by Grimsby fans, all the more so as there's been precious little success to speak of in the twelve years since. A respectable mid-table finish in 1998-99 followed, and then came a narrow escape from relegation back to the third tier. The directors were unhappy with the way things were shaping up, and just two league games into the ensuing 2000-01 season Buckley, the hero of two years earlier, was dismissed. He made way for the experienced Lennie Lawrence, who had just spent his first summer without work in 23 years as a manager, having been sacked by Luton Town.

Lawrence would last around sixteen months in charge of Grimsby before he eventually went the way of all managerial flesh in December 2001. He won fewer than a third of his 78 games at the helm. It would be grossly unfair to point the finger directly at Lawrence (indeed, many fans think he did a good job in tricky circumstances), but Grimsby's steady decline in modern times did seem to start in earnest during his era at Blundell Park. Therefore, our story begins here . . .

Chapter 1

Merry Christmas, Mr Lawrence!

Nationwide Football League	2001-02
Division One (level 2)	19th
FA Cup	3rd Round
League Cup	4th Round

If you are a football fan, and English, chances are you'll remember exactly where you were and how you felt on the night in 2001 when Sven Göran Eriksson's England larruped Germany 5-1 in their own backyard. And if you are a Grimsby supporter, it's even more likely.

For Saturday, 1 September 2001 was not only a sporting red-letter day for the nation, it was a day of celebration in north-east Lincolnshire too. Grimbarians, around 6,000 of them, saw their humble side rise to the top of the second level One for the first time in twenty years. Expensive new signing Phil Jevons scored his first goal for the Mariners with a sweet finish to see off Nigel Spackman's Barnsley, and there it was in black-and-white in all the papers the next day: Grimsby Town atop the table, officially the best side outside the FA Premier League.

It was a dizzying experience for even the most level-headed of Pontoonites, so perhaps it was just as well the euphoria only lasted 24 hours. The following day Burnley sneaked a late winner to overcome Bradford City 3-2 and the Clarets duly took over the top spot. Ah well, it was nice while it lasted.

Less than ten years after that famous day in 2001, Grimsby finds itself countless rungs further down the league ladder, welcoming the likes of Hayes & Yeading and Histon to Blundell Park for league matches. Who could have foreseen a decline of those proportions back in 2001? The slide downwards has been swift, clinical, and as chilling as the wind that blows into the ground off the North Sea.

Mariners fans could have been forgiven back then for thinking that maybe 2001-02 would prove a season in the sun. Big money had been spent on the team, and well-travelled old hand Lennie Lawrence was now properly settled in the manager's office. Surely the time had come to forget recent turmoil and discomfort? The previous campaign had seen Alan Buckley depart as manager early on – a real shock, as many thought he was almost unsackable – to be eclipsed by erudite Londoner Lawrence. Over his first few months the jury remained out on the new man.

Controversial team changes and baffling tactical formations abounded, and Grimsby only escaped relegation to the third tier of English football late in the campaign. It had not been a season of progress, with changes at board level destabilising things for a while, and the general atmosphere left many fans feeling anxious. People had become accustomed to what some labelled 'the boring Buckley years', with the same nucleus of players employing a rigid 4-4-2 formation and producing rather predictable fare.

The events of 1 September 2001 seemed to signal an end to all that. Now it was roller-coaster time. It was the first time Grimsby had topped English football's second tier since 1982, when a 4-1 pasting of Middlesbrough had done the trick. The key moment this time round came midway through the first half against Barnsley when locally born teenager Jonny Rowan surged impressively into the box and set up Phil Jevons to rifle the winner. The goalscorer had signed from Everton for a costly £250,000, and this was his first success in his fifth league match – the sighs of relief could be heard throughout South Humberside. After the goal, Grimsby had to defend for their lives to stay ahead, even after Barnsley goalkeeper Kevin Miller was sent off for bringing down Alan Pouton, ten yards outside his box. It had been a heavy collision and Pouton performed a rather flamboyant fall, but referee John Brandwood was adamant the Cornish custodian should depart, despite the visitors' fury at such an injustice.

This was the only game played in the top divisions that day, due to international call-ups affecting other clubs. The three points earned meant that Grimsby overtook Manchester City at the top, but as they had played one more game than the rest, it was inevitable that the stay in pole position would be short. In this case it would be barely 24 hours.

Never one for hyperbole or over-reaction, Lawrence acknowledged Grimsby's good fortune against Barnsley, particularly the sending off and a goal-line clearance by long-serving John McDermott, but added sagely that there would be plenty of days when Lady Luck would not favour them, so this was nothing to be embarrassed about. His opposite number, Spackman, moaned that his men had dominated, yet Grimsby only had one shot all game and scored with it.

It was certainly turning into a strange season, for despite their exalted position at the top, Grimsby had been flattened 2-4 at Fratton Park five days earlier, beaten by an extraordinary one-man show from Portsmouth's Robert Prosinecki, a 32-year-old Croatian. Prosinecki did his stuff despite reports he'd been out 'socialising' most of the previous night. Pompey fans in attendance would never forget that gloriously sunny bank holiday afternoon. Prosinecki took the Mariners apart with a breathtaking display of passing and artistry, the like of which home fans hadn't witnessed for years, if ever. He'd only debuted nine days earlier, but this was the day when English football realised what a craftsman Prosinecki really was. He sprayed long passes around for fun and contributed to all four of the goals that floored Grimsby. A heavy smoker known in his homeland as 'The Great Yellow One' (for his blond hair, not a lack of courage), Prosinecki became an instant folk hero that day, and went on to play a major role in saving Pompey from relegation, some of his tricks leaving even verbose Director of Football Harry Redknapp lost for words.

Grimsby may have been unable to get the ball off Prosinecki, but the two 1-0 wins that followed showed that no serious damage had been done to confidence or morale. When Jevons grabbed his second Grimsby goal – a cool chip following a howler by goalkeeper Magnus Hedman – to sink Coventry 1-0 at Highfield Road, the home side were plunged into such a state of gloom they promptly showed manager Gordon Strachan the door. Sky Blues fans had already been on Strachan's back for some time, and seeing their team beaten by humble Grimsby was apparently the final straw. Two or three hotheads invaded the pitch at the end and had to be physically pulled off Strachan, scenes which probably meant the Coventry board had little option but to part company with the little Scot. This was not the first time, nor would it be the last, that defeat by Grimsby has prompted an opposing club to sack their manager.

Mariners fans may have chuckled at the plight of Coventry, but little did they know their own season was about to take a turn for the worse from which it would never really recover, apart, that is, from one notable night in October (see 'Match of the Season' below).

Victory at Coventry was followed by a disastrous run of just one win in twenty games, a sequence that saw the Mariners in freefall from the top of the table to 23rd place by Christmas. Home attendances even slipped below 5,000 at one point. According to fans' website *The Electronic Fishcake*: 'Fewer people braved the dread – the slow, cold, clinging dread – of trudging up Cleethorpes Road and into the ground [on matchdays].'

Manager Lawrence, for all his experience, was seemingly at a loss over how to stop the rot. Nevertheless, there were surprisingly few calls for his head ('he was still very popular, mainly because he smiled a lot,' according to the *Fishcake*), with most fans apparently accepting he was being hampered by a harsh crop of injuries. Some preferred to blame the board for the malaise, for a perceived lack of financial support for their beleaguered manager.

A new low point was reached in mid-December with a 0-4 stuffing at fellow strugglers Walsall, where sections of the loyal away support were reduced to cheering for the home side and calling for more goals from them. A few left in disgust after the third goal went in. Walsall had sixteen goal-attempts to Grimsby's two and a more miserable 90 minutes was hard to recall. TV pundit Robbie Earle remarked that he'd never seen Lennie Lawrence (a league club manager of 985 games vintage) looking so down at the end of a match. It seemed the writing was on the wall, although the Grimsby directors were certainly in no hurry to sack Lawrence. They knew he was very popular with large sections of the fanbase, and basic decency demanded they didn't wield the axe just before Christmas.

Lawrence himself would say later that he never saw the sack coming, and it shook him to the core when his fate was revealed on the morning of Friday, 28 December. In the early editions of that day's *Grimsby Telegraph,* Lawrence was quoted that the following day's home game with Portsmouth would be 'make or break' as far as Town's survival prospects were concerned, even though there was still half a season left. But later editions of the same paper carried the wry headline 'Merry Christmas Mr Lawrence', announcing that the earlier rallying cry had come from the mouth of a dead man walking. Lawrence had become the 28th name on the list of ex-managers of Grimsby Town.

Lawrence revealed in his autobiography some years later that he was called in on the Friday and given the sack 'in a very professional way' and was assured it was nothing personal. He then had to head back to his lonely rented bungalow in the Lincolnshire countryside, throw a few bags into the back of his car and head south for his main home in Kent. But within an hour or two of his fate being broadcast on TV and radio, a new door was opening for the ex-Charlton, Middlesbrough, Bradford City and Luton manager, with Sam Hammam at Cardiff offering a position as Director of Football at Ninian Park, where Lawrence would assist and oversee rookie manager Alan Cork. It was a job Lawrence snapped up, and within a matter of weeks he was a manager again after Cork was deemed surplus to requirements. 'Twas ever thus on football's managerial merry-go-round.

Back at Blundell Park, Lawrence's erstwhile assistant, the local favourite John Cockerill, subsequently followed him out of the door, seemingly unhappy at not getting the main job himself. He was clearly unwilling to stay on as a mere assistant to the new player-manager Paul Groves. Cockerill appeared at least as popular as Lawrence, so chairman Peter Furneaux had to battle to prevent a PR disaster over all this, and he insisted the club pleaded 'around six times' with Cockerill to stay, without success. Cockerill disappeared over the horizon claiming he'd been sacked and it fell to former centre-half and Football in the Community officer Graham Rodger to become number two to Groves.

Back in the comfort of his native south-east, Lawrence told the press he had no intention of slagging off Grimsby in public – an understandable attitude as he still had six months remaining on a £150,000 annual contract and presumably expected a pay-off. Many fans shook their heads in dismay and lamented the departure of a man who'd been a breath of fresh air at the club just sixteen months earlier, when taking over a team mired in the negativity of the second Alan Buckley era. Opinion was divided over the suitability and readiness of the new boss Groves, with his sympathisers pointing out that he must be feeling 'like the man on the billows pump on the Titanic'.

It was widely felt the Grimsby board had gone for the cheap option by appointing two men already on the pay-roll. The purse strings were not being loosened often enough, cried the critics, and further evidence of this had come recently when three-month loanee Marlon Broomes went off to join Sheffield Wednesday when Grimsby weren't willing to meet his wage demands.

All this angst was a far cry from earlier, when the season had got off to a highly promising start. By now, however, it was clear that just 22 goals scored in 26 league games up to the point of Lawrence's departure was the root of the problem. Jevons, an expensive capture, had shown flashes of form but hadn't solved the club's goalscoring problem, and his promising partnership with young Jonny Rowan had been interrupted by injury.

It had been an autumn of almost unremitting misery, including a run of six successive losses in the league, and the only respite was a 3-1 win over managerless promotion-chasers Birmingham in late October. Jevons grabbed only his third league goal of the season that day, to add to two by speedy Mick Boulding, who had been snapped up on a free in September from Mansfield, and was starting only his second full game for the Mariners. Boulding, a 25-year-old Mancunian, might have even bagged a hat-trick but a third effort hit a post. Up to now, Boulding was better known for his exploits as a tennis player than as a winger. He'd been ranked among Britain's top twenty players, had roomed with Tim Henman, playing in tournaments around the globe, and just two years earlier had won ATP world ranking points.

Even the Birmingham victory had a downside, for Welsh international defender Alan Neilson, drafted in on loan from Fulham to replace long-term injury victim John McDermott, was injured himself. Following the six straight previous defeats, only 5,149 turned out to see the game, and a fair chunk of those were following the visitors. It would be another ten games before the next league victory came along, by which time relegation worries were overwhelming.

Having been hurriedly installed to replace Lawrence, Paul Groves' task on his first full day in the job was to turn the tide and overcome a talented but under-achieving mid-table Portsmouth side boasting Robert Prosinecki and Peter Crouch in its ranks. The rapid movement of events that weekend was underlined by the fact that the programme notes for this post-Christmas game came from the pen of Lennie Lawrence, who by now was hundreds of miles away sorting out his future in south Wales. Some fans turned up and voiced their anger at Lawrence's sacking, but generally a spirited performance against Pompey received the spirited reception it deserved. Crouch's first-half goal was cancelled out just before the interval as Town netted twice from corners, via Jevons and then the first goal of Simon Ford's career. In the second period Town attacked the Pontoon end with vigour, hit the underside of the bar and had two loud penalty appeals waved away before a linesman confirmed a third request – Jevons netting the spot-kick past Japanese goalkeeper Kawaguchi. It was a storming 3-1 victory and created hopes of a great escape from relegation, and afterwards a thrilled Graham Rodger magnanimously dedicated it to the departed Lawrence and Cockerill.

But despite all the gung-ho determination of the rookie management, the win over Pompey would prove a false dawn. Only two goals were scored in the next ten games, which included an embarrassing FA Cup exit to York City, when Town were frankly outclassed by the club 91st in the League. At least Groves was able to recruit some decent-looking loan signings, something Lawrence had largely been unable to do. These temporary trouble-shooters included Wolves forward Robert Taylor and Charlton pair Andy Todd and Martin Pringle. Unfortunately Taylor only lasted four games (featuring a goal, a sending off and an injury), while the Swede Pringle was hospitalised in only his second game.

Todd, son of the legendary Derby and England defender Colin, added some grit and know-how to the defence, while Pringle, a tall 31-year-old Swede, was a lively attacker who had three years' experience on Benfica's books. Blundell Park on a chilly Tuesday night in February presents quite a contrast to the Stadium of Light in Lisbon, and poor Pringle got a lot more than he bargained for when he trotted out to face Stockport in his first Mariners home game. A horrific tackle by long-throw expert Dave Challinor smashed Pringle's leg in two places below the knee. It was an ugly challenge which not only ended Pringle's stay with Grimsby, it ended his entire career in senior football. The irony was that he'd only agreed to come to Grimsby in order to regain some fitness, having spent much of his time at Charlton on the injured list, following an £800,000 move from Portugal.

The horror occurred shortly after half-time, with the Mariners already 3-1 up, and looking set for a third win under the control of Groves. Challinor's wild lunge ended with Pringle being rushed to the Diana, Princess of Wales Hospital in Grimsby. Groves and the other Grimsby players were furious about the tackle, and Stockport player-manager Carlton Palmer was quick to apologise to try and defuse things. Astonishingly, Challinor was not red-carded, so Palmer took matters into his own hands and substituted the player (and would later fine him a fortnight's wages too).

By the end of the game it was Palmer, rather than the irate Grimsby players, who had a running battle with referee Mark Clattenburg. Near the end Palmer sarcastically applauded one of his decisions and the official lost patience and sent him off. At the end of this stormy night, Grimsby had the three points they badly needed to kick-start a bid to avoid relegation, but for poor Pringle his entire career was hanging by a thread. He was subsequently given a squad number by Charlton for the following (2002-03) season, but within a few months had to give up the struggle to regain fitness. He later moved into coaching in his native Scandinavia.

A week after seeing off Stockport, play-off hopefuls Crystal Palace were thumped 5-2 at Blundell Park. Todd, who'd only managed one goal in 51 games at Charlton, rocketed a fine opener to add to the goal on his home debut. A fortnight later he was at it again, heading a late winner at high-flying Wolves, who had the notorious Aussie Kevin Muscat red-carded for illegally brandishing an elbow. A great escape from relegation was on the cards as the Mariners moved up to nineteenth (their best placing since the autumn) with a 6-2 hammering of Wimbledon. A lively half-time team talk from Groves did the trick this time, for the scores were level at the break. Town's cause was again aided by a sending-off, visiting goalkeeper Ian Feuer red-carded for felling Boulding when the score was still 3-2.

Lennie Lawrence had only chalked up five wins in 26 league games before his dismissal, but Groves managed to engineer seven in twenty to steer Grimsby clear of the trap door. Safety was assured with a 3-1 win over Burnley, the in-form Boulding grabbing another two. Consequently a season of trial and tribulation ended with smiles all round, the Mariners finishing on 50 points and two points clear of the drop. At one stage they had been six adrift of the safety level and looking bound for Division Two, with the green shoots of recovery only really emerging in late February. Key factors were the recruitment of Andy Todd, a run of seven goals in the final seven weeks from Boulding, plus of course the implosion of Crewe, who only won once in their final dozen games.

Match of the Season 2001-02

LIVERPOOL 1 GRIMSBY 2   Worthington Cup, 9 October 2001

Considerably more than 6,000 Grimsby fans trekked westwards to Merseyside for the club's biggest game in several years. Sadly, seven first-teamers were unavailable and it was a somewhat makeshift line-up that faced Gerard Houllier's glamour-boys in the third round of the Worthington Cup. If we play Liverpool ten times, warned Lennie Lawrence, they will win eight, one will be drawn and we might win one. And if that wasn't enough to bring the optimists back down to earth, they only had to look at the Grimsby line-up, full of square pegs jammed into round holes, due to the injury list. To cap it all, Lawrence confessed he'd been to Anfield five times in 23 years as a manager, and all he'd ever got was a cup of tea and a nice chat.

Having lowered everybody's expectations levels, Lawrence then watched with pride as his rearranged team produced one of Grimsby's finest hours, a tremendous giant-killing act against a team containing eight internationals, a couple of Under-21 caps, and with England's current centre-forward on the bench.

In a nutshell, Town withstood an onslaught and then nicked a winner in the last seconds of extra-time. Phil Jevons' 35-yard winner was one of the greatest goals ever seen at this famous ground, reckoned the *Grimsby Telegraph*. The wonder-goal had produced Grimsby's first win in 24 attempts at this ground, dating back to 1892, and they hadn't even scored here since 1958. The 32,000 gate was bigger than anticipated and provided the bonus of a £125,000 windfall for the hard-up visitors.

The performance was a marvellous response to the criticism incurred for a dreadful home display five days earlier, in a defeat by Rotherham. Liverpool were held at bay thanks to resolute defending and at half-time Grimsby received a standing ovation from their proud travelling fans. They returned to hold firm for another 45 minutes, and were unlucky not to win a penalty themselves in the 90th minute when Sammy Hyppia appeared to pull sub Boulding. Into extra-time it went, and finally the stout resistance ended when loanee defender David Beharall handled and Gary McAllister netted a penalty for the Reds with 101 minutes on the clock.

But instead of the floodgates opening, Grimsby hit back to grab a shock equaliser, Stuart Campbell's cross fired in by Marlon Broomes with seven minutes remaining. A penalty shoot-out was on the cards as the game entered its dying moments, and manager Lawrence could be seen deep in discussion with assistant Cockerill over who should take them. As they pencilled down the names, a long punt forward by keeper Danny Coyne was headed down by Hyppia and collected by Jevons, who steadied himself and clipped an absolute beauty from distance into the top left-hand corner past the diving figure of Chris Kirkland. It was a classic smash-and-grab, last-gasp winner – and right in front of the massed Grimsby fans too.

Jevons, of course, had recently signed from nearby Everton, grew up locally, and had Liverpool fans in his immediate family. He'd even been rejected by the Reds as a schoolboy after being on their books for two years. His parents David and Barbara were watching excitedly from high in the stands. It was the perfect end to a perfect night, with the icing on the cake being the standing ovation for the Town players from the generous Liverpool fans.

And so Grimsby went through to the last sixteen, the draw giving them another mouth-watering big night out, this time at the home of either Manchester United or Arsenal, whose third round game was to be played several weeks later. These two big guns fielded under-strength sides for their tie, the Gunners winning 4-0 to provide 4,000 Mariners fans with a trip to north London. Arsène Wenger again put out a virtual reserve side for Grimsby's visit, but it still contained £6 million Brazilian Edu and £13 million Frenchman Sylvain Wiltord, who struck the two goals that won the day. Grimsby's joint-best League Cup run in seventeen years was over, but would never be forgotten.

Chapter 2

'Bedlam, Absolute Bedlam . . .'

Nationwide Football League	2002-03
Division One (level 2)	24th (relegated)
FA Cup	3rd Round
League Cup	1st Round

It's a sad reflection on the state of our national game that whenever we take a look back at how smaller clubs fared in the first decade of the 21st century, there is no avoiding the influence exerted by money – or rather the lack of it – which followed the great ITV Digital crash of 2002.

The money-spinning ITV deal to broadcast games outside the Premiership had been seen as a life-saver for the hard-up clubs like Grimsby *et al*. Rubbing their hands with glee at the windfalls coming their way, many clubs had budgeted ahead with confidence. But the deal negotiated with the League would prove one financial burden too many for ITV Digital, and it slid into administration in March 2002, ceasing to be altogether a few weeks later. The collapse spelt big trouble for football.

Scores of clubs were left in serious financial straits, some unable to pay players, now that promised cash was not to be forthcoming. Some clubs had already invested in ground improvements, others had bought players and offered contracts they could now ill-afford. The effect was that certain clubs went into administration, a fate that didn't quite befall Grimsby, who plugged on and cut their cloth accordingly. The lack of funds certainly made life difficult for player-manager Paul Groves in his first full season in charge. The Football League went to court to try and claw some of the money back though litigation, but it was ultimately unsuccessful.

Grimsby chairman Peter Furneaux confirmed the club was in dire straits but promised a healthy new sponsorship deal was on the way to help out. He also intimated that the club had approached the PFA to discuss if and how they could renegotiate the current contracts of the players in view of what had happened. The latter was naturally unwelcome news in the dressing room and one unnamed player told the *Grimsby Telegraph* that if the board thought any contracted player would agree to a pay cut, they had another think coming.

It was clear Grimsby had stretched themselves financially in recent years in order to survive alongside the bigger clubs in Division One, and would find it hard to cope with the withdrawal of the TV money, which wiped out an estimated 55 per cent of projected income. Swingeing cost-cutting would have to follow, and sure enough Groves' squad was reduced to the bare bones. Coaches at the local School of Excellence lost their jobs and a brand new youth development system was launched. It looked like the board was trying to do the impossible: save money while increasing the volume of locally grown talent. The inevitable departure of the best players began with Danny Butterfield and Michael Boulding joining Crystal Palace and Aston Villa, respectively, with Danny Coyne and Phil Jevons being put on the transfer list.

Groves had to wheel and deal to get a squad together and was not helped by early injures when the 2002-03 season got underway. A 0-4 hammering at Norwich on the opening day was followed by a sickening injury to striker Steve Livingstone in the 1-2 home defeat by Derby. 'Livvo' sustained a fractured skull in an incident which held the game up for fifteen minutes, and would be out of action for a matter of months rather than weeks. This miserable start to the campaign extended until near the end of September, with two draws and seven defeats making up the opening nine league games.

The atmosphere of doom and gloom was not helped when local radio alleged the club could go bust, due to a £500,000 tax bill, a situation the chairman denied. Club records of the wrong sort were being broken by the lack of victories, but Groves promised he was not a quitter, and that things would improve.

Some light did indeed appear at the end of the tunnel after a 2-1 win at fellow-strugglers Brighton, but quickly vanished at the subsequent home match with Reading, a 0-3 defeat described by some observers as the worst display in at least fifteen years.

Livingstone returned to the fray three days later for the visit of Ipswich and the presence of this cult hero, plus Ipswich's inability to deal with the searing pace of Steve Kabba, helped the Mariners spring a surprisingly comfortable 3-0 win. A day or two later the Ipswich board reacted by sacking George Burley, their manager of eight years. And there was more encouraging news at the end of October when a thoroughly surreal 6-5 win over Burnley (see 'Match of the Season' below) was followed by locally produced John Oster returning to Blundell Park on loan. A winger or midfielder, Oster had left Grimsby in his teens in exchange for nearly £2 million from Everton in 1997, and later moved to Sunderland for another seven-figure fee. But Oster's career was now at something of a crossroads following an unfortunate episode when an air-rifle accidentally went off in his flat, causing bad damage to the eye of a team-mate, and ending his career as a result. The fans were glad to see him back in Grimsby colours, and he obliged with a goal in a 1-1 draw with Gillingham on his return.

Town remained in the bottom four up to and beyond Christmas 2002, a position they had occupied since the first league table of the season was calculated. And when January and February produced just one win from nine games in all, even the most optimistic Poontoonite was ready to throw in the towel.

Groves used the new relaxed rules about loan signings as best he could and, in total, 33 different players were employed in league fixtures over the season, but it remained backs-to-the-wall stuff throughout. Results in early March conspired to send Grimsby to a rock-bottom 24th, but they were never completely cut off from the rest and the dog-fight at the bottom remained as intense as ever. Eight valuable points were gained from four games in a twelve-day period in mid-March, but all the good work appeared to be undone when this little run was followed by three successive defeats.

It all boiled down to D-day arriving on Easter Monday, when Walsall were visitors to Blundell Park. A goalless draw with relegation rivals Sheffield Wednesday 48 hours earlier had left Grimsby hot favourites to drop – and this would be confirmed by 5pm unless Grimsby beat Walsall and Stoke lost at Coventry. Even then, the agony might only be prolonged a week longer.

As it was, Grimsby lost by a scrappy 0-1 and were down. It was a poor game and Grimsby looked tactically inept, succumbing to a goal just after the break that was a comedy of errors, scored by the Brazilian Junior. A bad pass by Tony Gallimore was not cleared despite several opportunities to do so, and Jorge Leitao's shot was brilliantly parried by Coyne, only for the ball to fall to Junior, who lashed it home off the underside of the bar in spectacular fashion. Ian Roper then nearly donated sad Grimsby an own-goal when his header sailed over his own keeper but hit the bar. There was to be no escape this time, Grimsby ending bottom of Division One.

Player-manager Groves ripped off his shirt at the final whistle and sprinted straight down the tunnel, a move that brought him criticism for not acknowledging the fans. Among the miserable onlookers was match-ball sponsor for the day Austin Mitchell, MP. Exactly a year earlier the Right Honourable Member for Great Grimsby had double cause for celebration – the Mariners avoiding relegation, plus his silver jubilee anniversary as an MP – but on this grim day he and 4,617 others had precious little to smile about.

Match of the Season 2002-03

GRIMSBY 6 BURNLEY 5   Division One, 29 October 2002

Assistant manager Graham Rodger called before this game for some 'Grimsby grit' to overcome the mid-table Clarets. He got a lot more than he bargained for. From a distinctly unpromising scenario (the two teams had managed only 32 goals in 33 games between them thus far) 5,200 home fans and 400 visitors were served up a rip-roaring goal feast. It would be the first time eleven goals had ever been scored in a league game at Blundell Park, and Grimsby became the only club to have won games by 6-5 both home and away, the latter occurring 70 years earlier at West Bromwich Albion.

In view of the date of the game, it turned into something of a hal-lowe'en nightmare for those who appreciate the finer arts of defending. But in all other respects it was a night to savour. The fun began with only 150 seconds on the clock as flying winger Steve Kabba lashed in Darren Barnard's cross, but by halfway through the first-half Stan Ternent's men had hauled themselves back into it, Gareth Taylor pouncing to head into the corner of the net.

Six minutes further on came the goal that the Grimsby faithful had yearned for, ever since the horrendous head injury suffered by popular Steve Livingstone ten weeks earlier against Derby. Barnard clipped a cross to the far post, where Livingstone met the ball with his head inside the six-yard box, the crowd holding its breath as it slowly looped out of the reach of goalkeeper Marlon Beresford and into the bottom corner. The roar that greeted the goal must have halted the tide on the nearby beach, and cult hero Livingstone responded by embracing his fans behind the goal. He admitted later that when that goal went in and another eight followed it, he wondered if he was suffering some sort of relapse fol-lowing his fractured skull in August.

Within two minutes the cheers were silenced as Burnley's Ian Moore netted a second equaliser from close range, but it was only a matter of seconds before the lead was restored to 3-2, Kabba sliding in to convert a deflected cross. Stuart Campbell prodded the ball home at the far post to extend the lead but, in added time, with the Grimsby bench furiously demanding that referee Paul Danson sound his whistle, Robbie Blake rat-tled a glorious low drive into the home net to give a bizarre interval score-line of 4-3.

Scoring so close to the changearound always seems to inspire a team, and sure enough Burnley came out with their tails up and duly equalised within a few minutes of the restart, Taylor ramming in a cross following a fine solo run by Moore. But this was no ordinary match, and their joy wouldn't last, McGregor handling a Livingstone cross less than ten minutes later for Pouton to net from the penalty spot. With nearly twenty minutes still remaining, Grimsby scored again from their very first corner of the game, their sixth goal from seven attempts on goal thus far. This time the stooping Ford did the honours to nod home.

Burnley were not finished by any means, and when Barnard brought down Papadopoulos seven minutes from time, Blake stepped up to score from the spot and make it 6-5. By tonight's standards there was still plenty of time to grab an equaliser, particularly when four minutes of added time was indicated, and the visitors laid siege to the Grimsby goal. At one point a melee broke out near the touchline as Grimsby tried to retain possession and run down the clock. The wrestling and the football were both allowed to continue by the unusually lenient Mr Danson, and Burnley went within a whisker of breaking clear to level matters yet again. The excellent *Cod Almighty* website would later describe the frantic final moments of this extraordinary night as: 'Bedlam, absolute bedlam . . . just noise, no discernible words, just a primeval scream.'

It had been a great spectacle and – in time-honoured fashion – the managers and coaches trotted out the usual stuff about shambolic defending, when perhaps they should have concentrated more on the excellent entertainment and lethal finishing. When the dust had settled, Grimsby were left to reflect on the fact that a huge amount of work was still needed to climb the table, for they'd still only gained twelve points and scored sixteen goals in sixteen games, even including tonight's rich pickings.

Chapter 3

'Lying in Tatters and Rags . . .'

Nationwide Football League	2003-04
Division Two (level 3)	21st (relegated)
FA Cup	2nd Round
League Cup	1st Round
Football League Trophy	1st Round

It had been a baptism of fire for tenacious player-manager Paul Groves, but relegation in his first season in charge didn't result in the sack, for there were mitigating circumstances. The serious shortage of funds at Blundell Park had meant he could rarely go shopping, and even then it was only to the bargain basement. Building a squad to compete seriously with the likes of Portsmouth, Sheffield United and Wolves was something of a non-starter, and when the inevitable crop of injuries occurred, he'd found himself down to the bare bones.

On paper the stats for the 2002-03 season had looked dreadful – just nine wins and 85 goals conceded – but the directors were prepared to give Groves another crack at it, with the Mariners now back in football's third tier. Such is the way of football, however, it was clear that a good 2003-04 season would be absolutely essential if he wanted to prolong his fledgling managerial career.

It was rumoured that the collapse of ITV Digital in 2002 had left Grimsby floundering with debts of more than £2 million, substantial chunks of which were owed to the Inland Revenue and to the club's bankers. Established players like goalkeeper Danny Coyne, defender and player of the year Georges Santos, and striker Steve Livingstone were among the twelve men consequently taken off the wage bill and shipped out in the summer of 2003, ending up at Leicester, Ipswich and Carlisle, respectively.

Another sign of the times was the club effectively having to supply its own kit, branded 'Grimsby Town Sports' following the closure of long-serving supplier Avec Sportswear. The new faces arriving at Blundell Park included a pair of Dutchmen in Laurens Ten Heuvel and Marcel Cas, both recruited from Sheffield United, midfielder Des Hamilton from Cardiff, and Portsmouth defender Jason Crowe. Goalkeeper Aidan Davison returned for a second spell in Grimsby colours, while striker Phil Jevons was back after a long loan at neighbours Hull City, where he'd only managed three goals in 24 league games. On paper, at least, it looked the sort of squad that should at least be able to hold its own in the third tier, and seven points garnered from the opening four games seemed to back this view.

However, as the long summer evenings gave way to autumn's chill, the skies began to darken ominously over Blundell Park. Perhaps the first signs that all was not well came from behind the scenes, when the club reacted badly to negative coverage in the local paper, the *Grimsby Telegraph*. In early September it was revealed that the club was withdrawing recognition (i.e. banning) reporter Stuart Rowson for what it called 'continued misleading coverage of the club'. Rowson could no longer speak to any staff at the ground and had his press pass withdrawn. The ban was implemented after a front-page splash in which the paper reported that Grimsby Town had stopped paying for an ambulance to stand by at Blundell Park for any emergencies on matchdays, in a bid to save money. The paper confirmed its editor had been invited to Blundell Park to discuss the situation, but said it wouldn't attend unless the reporter's rights were reinstated. It all seemed very petty and probably something of a PR own-goal by the club.

Shortly after this row became public, the Mariners were due to face Hartlepool in a Friday night away game. The *Telegraph* was published at lunchtime with page 7 of its matchday supplement completely blank, instead of being filled with pre-match news as was the norm. The town's MP Austin Mitchell, a journalist by trade himself, said banning the reporter had been a retrograde step by the club. He said the club should not bully the local press or deal with negative coverage in this petulant way. Several weeks later the paper would apologise for being misleading with its ambulance story, but it was an episode from which nobody emerged smiling.

That night on the pitch Grimsby caved in and suffered their worst defeat on the field in 55 years, Hartlepool romping to an 8-1 success. Eight goals had not been shipped in a single game since the Mariners bade farewell to the top division in 1948 with a last-day 0-8 thrashing at Highbury by champions Arsenal. For the hardy 272 who travelled up to Victoria Park, it really was Black Friday, the heaviest defeat in most of their lifetimes. Player-manager Groves was mortified and apologised publicly to the travelling fans for what they had witnessed. He attached no blame to the two YTS youngsters who featured, David Soames and Liam Nimmo, but blamed the more experienced men, who had defended like schoolboys. Presumably he included himself in that criticism, for he would drop himself for the subsequent game.

It was a game between two mid-table clubs and nobody expected the slaughter that unfolded. Believe it or not, the match was still goalless after nineteen minutes, at which point Groves netted an embarrassing own-goal, nodding the ball past the indecisive figure of Davison. A mere 90 seconds later Simon Ford stumbled at a vital moment and then tripped the 35-year-old veteran poacher Marco Gabbiadini. Paul Robinson, a player rejected by Grimsby a year earlier, stepped up to net the penalty. After a misdemeanour by Darren Barnard, Gavin Strachan lashed home the third Hartlepool goal from a free-kick, and then Richie Humphreys buried another for 4-0. A Jonny Rowan tap-in shortly after half-time made it 4-1, producing some rather ironic-sounding cheers from the Grimsby fans. But Ford's nightmare continued when he then under-hit a back-pass and Robinson nipped in to grab his second and Hartlepool's fifth. On the hour mark, Robinson was left in acres of space to set up Gabbiadini for 1-6 and before long Eifion Williams had tapped in from a Gabbiadini pass to increase the misery. To round things off, Grimsby old boy Robinson converted a simple chance to complete a satisfying hat-trick.

A week later and, following a 1-2 home reverse to Swindon, Grimsby responded by hammering a very poor Chesterfield outfit 4-0 at Blundell Park, the celebrations for one of the goals leading to an extraordinary punch-up between Mariners team-mates Darren Barnard and Tony Crane. Grimsby had already had three players sent off this season, but escaped punishment this time, although the duo did find themselves fined by their manager a few days later. The Chesterfield romp meant Grimsby fans had witnessed sixteen goals in three games, but any renewed optimism would be blasted out of the water in the following weeks during which the side could only bag one goal – a second-half winner at Blackpool – in its next four league encounters. Form was very scratchy and by the end of October 2003 the season's tally was six wins, six defeats and a mood of mid-table mediocrity.

Nevertheless, Michael Boulding found himself among the goals and looked the part, even though collectively Grimsby failed to impress as the halfway point of the season beckoned. Jason Crowe didn't help by earning himself a long suspension for stamping on a Bournemouth opponent. In attack, the forwards were beginning to misfire so regularly that Phil Jevons was finally given his starting place back at Christmas and he responded with two superb goals in a 3-3 Boxing Day draw with Oldham. But Grimsby then managed to go through December and January without a single victory. It meant a relegation battle once again beckoned. There was little light relief during these dark weeks, but straight-talking defender Tony Crane startled a few with his unusual verdict that Jevons' well-taken goals against Oldham had been 'different gravy'. It was one for Mariners' fans to ponder.

The new year of 2004 only heralded more gloom in its opening weeks at Blundell Park, with injuries, rumours that Michael Boulding and Alan Pouton were about to be sold, and heavy defeats at Wycombe and Port Vale to boot. Morale was dented yet further when big defender Marcel Cas walked out of the club after a bust-up with Groves, returning to his native Holland. Cas rejoined former club RBC Rosendaal, complaining he'd been played out of position at Blundell Park. He said when he first joined Town he had been promised 'a small club with a big ambition, being taken forward by a fresh young manager'. This had not been the case, he suggested.

Poor Groves was getting stick from all quarters but to his credit he refused to trade insults with Cas through the press. Rumours that Groves had been urged by his chairman to forget playing and concentrate on the managing side of his job only added to the pressure. A midweek 1-3 home defeat by Wrexham in front of a paltry, frozen stiff, and dispirited crowd of 3,572 then put Groves' future in ever more serious doubt. It was Town's eighth successive league game without a win, they'd dropped to a miserable twentieth in the table, and the writing appeared to be on the wall.

With matches postponed due to bad weather, there was a nineteen-day winter hiatus, but instead of using the time to regroup and make a fresh start, Grimsby got caught up in a bitter war of words over the future of leading scorer Boulding. Coveted by a number of clubs, notably Barnsley, he seemed certain to leave, but chairman Peter Furneaux was determined to wait for the right deal to come along. Despite being urged to concentrate on managing, 38-year-old Groves couldn't resist picking himself for the February game at Oldham Athletic, only his seventh start of the season. Those who reckoned this would all end in tears would soon be proved correct.

The match was played on a Sunday by special request of the home club, who called the occasion 'Celebration Sunday', their way of marking their emergence from administration and the formation of a new company to run the club. Attractions included free admission, dancing girls and all manner of extra-curricular activities designed to put a smile back on Latics fans' faces. This helped persuade a bumper turnout of 1,100 Grimsby fans to make the trip across the Pennines, most of whom would subsequently wish they hadn't bothered. Oldham were five goals to the good by half-time, with Grimsby down to ten men, having had defender

Mike Edwards red-carded. The players trooped gloomily off at the inter-val with chants of 'We want Grovesy out' and 'You're not fit to wear the shirt' ringing in their ears. For the second half, Groves wisely subbed himself and Oldham went on to make it six goals without reply, by which time many Mariners' fans had left the stadium. One estimate reckoned just 300 of the 1,100 remained by the end.

The following day, the inevitable took place and Groves was relieved of his duties, with Graham Rodger again placed in temporary charge, and Grimsby looking for their 25th post-war manager. The chairman announced that Groves would remain as a player, but this odd notion was soon squashed when the player called in the PFA to help him negotiate the end of his playing contract.

Rodger rang the changes and was able to find a winning formula immediately with a rousing 2-1 victory over promotion-chasing Brighton. His stint in charge would last seven games, and he helped inspire three valuable wins in all, including a highly unexpected 6-1 romp against mid-table Barnsley which featured four goals and a missed penalty from Jevons, to add to the brace he notched against Luton four days earlier. It raised fresh hope of an escape from relegation, moving Town clear of the bottom four, but was not quite enough to get Rodger the job full-time. Forty-two-year-old former Chesterfield and Bradford City boss Nicky Law was introduced as the new manager on 4 March.

Law quickly got busy in the transfer market and brought in veterans Paul Warhurst, Alan Fettis and Jamie Lawrence, the well-travelled forward Mickael Antoine-Curier, and injury-prone Huddersfield midfielder John Thorrington. French striker Antoine-Curier was appearing for his ninth English club at the age of only 21, which left Grimsby fans wondering why he'd been unable to settle or impress at the other eight. Sadly he failed to get among the goals at Blundell Park and, apart from a thrilling 4-4 draw at Chesterfield, Grimsby's season tailed off disappointingly, leaving them still teetering on the fringe of the relegation zone at the beginning of May. It was exactly the position Law had been detailed to avoid.

Match of the Season 2003-04

Tranmere 2 Grimsby 1   Division Two, 8 May 2004

And so it all came down to this, Grimsby's day of destiny, the final 90 minutes of a trouble-torn season. A win at Prenton Park today would be enough to keep them up, no matter how results panned out elsewhere. Grimsby's future was in their own hands, but to win here was a tough call – they hadn't won away from home in nearly six months.

Even more worrying, Tranmere's form was awesome. Although they had lost 1-2 at Port Vale last time out, they had won seven of the previous eight, drawn the other, and were cursing the fact that their late surge had arrived too late to carry them into the play-offs.

Events at Chesterfield and Rushden would also affect the relegation situation, but Law and his men had to forget about the possible permutations and simply go all out for a win. Around 2,000 noisy Mariners fans headed for the Wirral and nervous chairman Peter Furneaux got amongst them, wandering around the pitch with director John Fenty to applaud and encourage their boisterous contribution in the Cowshed End. A giant flag was unfurled and was passed around, jostling for space with the array of inflatable Harry Haddocks and other piscatorial memorabilia.

Roared on enthusiastically, Town's great escape got underway according to plan when Darren Mansaram put them ahead on 24 minutes, converting a low driven cross from the lively Isiah Rankin. The lead was still intact at half-time, at which point, with all the League One scores taken into account, Grimsby were an optimistic eighth from the bottom of the table. For that happy situation to be maintained it would need no further change to the scorelines at Prenton Park, Saltergate and Nene Park, to mention but three, by 5pm.

Grimsby hung on tenaciously, but either side of the hour mark came the three incidents that would prove pivotal. First, Tranmere's David Beresford fired over a cross which was converted by Iain Hume's far-post header to level the scores. Then, renewed cause for Grimsby optimism as Rovers defender Ian Sharps was sent off after receiving a second yellow card for holding back Mansaram. But, perversely, this only inspired Brian Little's men, who had nothing to play for except pride and a win bonus, and they quickly burst into the lead, Eugene Dadi springing Grimsby's offside trap to stroke his shot home. With less than twenty minutes of the season left to save themselves, Town raised their game, boosted, no doubt, by a huge cheer from Grimsby fans receiving favourable news on their radios and mobile phones that Bury had taken the lead at Rushden.

As the minutes ticked by and it became clear an equaliser was unlikely, the mood in the crowded Cowshed sank lower. Even with ten men Tranmere looked the better side and Grimsby were going to need events elsewhere to keep them up. But the dream died when, in the 88th minute at Saltergate, Glynn Hurst broke the deadlock to net a late goal for Chesterfield against mid-table Luton. Unless Grimsby now scored twice in the dying seconds – a draw would not be enough – the Spireites would leapfrog them into twentieth place. Rushden & Diamonds were now 0-2 down and were surely out of it.

Clive Penton blew the final whistle and the instant mood of deflation told the story; no need to wait for confirmation from Saltergate – Grimsby were back in the bottom division. There was much mourning and gnashing of teeth, the usual tears, embraces and periods of stunned silence. The Tranmere players then did an end-of-season lap of honour and shared mutual applause with the Grimsby fans in a surprisingly dignified final cameo. A handful of the Grimsby players acknowledged their superb fans at the final whistle, but Law and Rankin, in particular, were in no mood for a lap of honour and headed straight down the tunnel. It was probably an understandable reaction, but one which drew fierce criticism from disgruntled fans. One of them, soldier Craig Bray, had spent several hundred pounds getting to the game from his base in Germany and when pressed later was highly critical of the squad for not re-emerging from their dressing room of shame.

Another long-standing fan, the *Cod Almighty* website reporter Tony Butcher, attempted to put in words the sheer misery of the moment: 'Strung out behind us were the banners and flags proclaiming defiance, but the Town team, like the season, lies in tatters and rags. All our pretensions laid bare: we're back in the third, we are a third division team. Once upon a time we were dragged up from the gutter through tough love, and now we're back in it like a recidivist, an alcoholic. You don't know what you've got 'til it's gone. Still, we'll be back. Somewhere, someday, somehow.'

When all was done and dusted, the final table showed Grimsby in 21st position, just a point behind Chesterfield. Had Hurst not netted against Luton, the Mariners would have survived. More than 90 goals conceded during the campaign was the most damning Grimsby statistic, although nine red cards and three different managers were not exactly minor issues. Reflecting on their second successive relegation, chairman Furneaux said the two-year period had been disastrous and this decline simply had to be stopped. Today's outcome had cost the club £500,000, he estimated.

Grimsby now knew what it was like to drop two divisions in two seasons. Not many clubs or their supporters have endured that kind of misery. Ironically, in the early 1990s, the Mariners had enjoyed the opposite sensation, successive promotions between the same divisions. They had been accompanied by Southend and Cambridge United in their rise from Fourth to Second Division, the only time in Football League history that three clubs have climbed two divisions in harness with each other.

The drop to the basement meant the end of the line for Nicky Law, whose short stay at the helm ended within a few days of the final game. His contract was not renewed when it expired on 10 May. He was followed out of the door by no fewer than fourteen players as Grimsby began cutting their cloth in readiness for the new surroundings ahead. Law had a managerial CV that included eleven straight wins in charge of Chesterfield, but at Grimsby he'd only conjured up three wins and two draws from twelve games. He would end up joining non-league Buxton. Before the month of May was out, the vacant post at Blundell Park had been filled by 43-year-old Scarborough boss Russell Slade, hardly a household name, but a man respected for his coaching work at Northampton, Notts County and Sheffield United. Perhaps more importantly, he had shown at Scarborough an ability to cope well with a small squad and little money.

Chapter 4

Back in the Basement

Coca-Cola Football League   2004-05
Division Two (level 4)   18th
FA Cup   1st Round
League Cup   2nd Round
Football League Trophy   1st Round

Grimsby were back down among the dead men, so to speak, for the start of the new season, condemned to be basement dwellers for the first time since 1990. New manager Russell Slade's task was demanding but simple – he not only had to halt the recent decline, but do so with a completely new playing squad of his own construction. He went about it with gusto, only a handful of familiar faces surviving from the previous season. New managers often favour bringing in their own people anyway, but this was a revolution that was forced upon Slade, whether he liked it or not. Many players left the club in the summer on the expiry of their contracts, meaning it was not so much a deliberate cull, but more a mass exodus.

Forty-four-year-old Slade was a curious appointment by the Grimsby board. He was certainly not the household name that some fans craved, but in twenty years had coped with some tough footballing challenges and was certainly up for the task of halting the serious slump in the Mariners' recent fortunes. Born in Surrey, he was one of those rarities in football – a manager with no playing experience at senior level – although not the first to be appointed at Grimsby, for Lawrie McMenemy and Lennie Lawrence had also never played in the Football League.

Slade had started out as a young PE teacher in Nottingham, learning the rudiments of coaching during a stint as a part-time assistant youth coach at Notts County in the 1980s. His involvement at Meadow Lane increased over the years and he eventually rose through the ranks to land full-time coaching work. He became right-hand man to manager Mick Walker, and then took over as caretaker-manager when Walker was sacked in 1994. Walker was succeeded by Howard Kendall four months later and Slade stayed on as Kendall's assistant. However, this new management team were shown the door after only a few months as County headed for relegation from Division One. Slade then joined the Sheffield Untied coaching staff, where he served as assistant manager and had two short spells as caretaker manager.

He finally made a manager's job his own aged 41 when taking over at Nationwide Conference crisis club Scarborough in 2001. They were adrift at the bottom and looking doomed but he guided them to a remarkable run that ensured safety and the following season had them riding high near the top of the table. But in early 2003, two days after that club went into administration, Slade reluctantly handed in his resignation. Presented with a fans' petition urging him to stay, a tearful Slade promptly did a U-turn, but the off-field troubles helped scupper Scarborough's promotion bid that year. The following season featured a long FA Cup run which was only ended by Claudio Ranieri's Premiership title-chasers Chelsea. Four months after this, Slade found himself Blundell Park-bound.

Just a week or two after being installed at Grimsby, Slade found himself working under a new chairman when businessman John Fenty, 42, took over that role from 58-year-old Peter Furneaux, who stood down after two stints in the chair. Grimsby-born Furneaux had been at the helm of his home-town club for seven years before selling his shares to Bill Carr in 1994, but became chairman again in 2001 when buying the majority stake from Doug Everitt for an undisclosed sum. His successor, Fenty, also locally born, was another man with the Mariners in his blood, a lifelong fan with considerable business acumen, judging by the success of his company Five Star Fish, which he'd built from scratch and was recently sold for £20 million.

The team which took the field for Grimsby's opening fixture (a 0-1 defeat at Darlington) included only two men who had featured the previous season – Jason Crowe and Darren Mansaram. The squad had basically been assembled from triallists and out-of-contract players looking for new clubs. Slade inherited just five men tied to Grimsby with a contract, and, of those, Iain Anderson soon left for Dundee and Tony Crane suffered a serious knee injury. It meant the team was jam-packed with mystery men so far as Grimsby fans were concerned at the first home match, a Tuesday night affair with Boston. New boy Michael Reddy rose from the subs' bench to score within a few minutes of his entrance, thus squaring the scores at the first Football League derby between the two clubs. The goal saved Town from an embarrassing home defeat and the home crowd quickly fell in love with Reddy.

When this son of Kilkenny had emerged at Sunderland he was described by Peter Reid as the most exciting prospect he'd ever worked with, but his career had by now stalled somewhat, and he was looking for a club at which to settle and perform regularly. His progress had been seriously hampered by a serious knee injury picked up in training, and in

the last three years or so he'd been loaned by the Wearsiders to five different clubs. Grimsby fans liked the look of him, and once they'd seen
fellow signings Andy Parkinson, Dean Gordon and Ashley Sestanovich
in action too, there was grudging praise for Slade's wheeling and dealing
in the transfer market. He may have been forced to scrape a few barrels
due to the shortage of cash, but these looked real bargains.

The glimpses of unfulfilled promise in those opening two games blos-
somed into a rousing victory in the third encounter, an astonishing half-
time turnaround at home to Bury sparking a 5-1 victory (see 'Match of
the Season' below). Star of the show was new signing Thomas Pinault
from Colchester, a French-born midfielder of great industry and no
mean skill. Pinault had had unsuccessful trials with Northampton and
Dundee United before Slade snapped him up. Slade seemed to favour a
3-4-3 formation in the opening weeks, and new boy Gordon, on the left
of the back three, impressed in this set-up, his experience just what
Grimsby needed in this hour of need. As a 31-year-old with experience
at five different clubs in higher divisions, Gordon was something of an
old hand, a man with more than a dozen England Under-21 caps to his
name, not forgetting 200-plus games on the books of Crystal Palace.

Hartlepool's Anthony Williams breezed into town to fill the boots of
genial Geordie custodian Aidan Davison who headed south to Colchester
– the fifteenth club of a peripatetic career involving two separate stints at
Blundell Park. Williams, although several years younger, could almost
match Davison, as he'd performed for eleven clubs, most of them involving loan spells. He was a multi-capped Welsh Under-21 international who
had started out at Blackburn. He would hold his place in the Grimsby
goal despite being guilty of a few high-profile errors – by no means the
only offender as the new-look side struggled to gel properly during the
autumn.

The optimism generated by the 5-1 hammering of Bury gradually dis-
sipated due to highly frustrating inconsistency in the subsequent weeks.
Encouraging victories would inevitably be followed by a defeat and, no
matter how he tried, Slade could not inspire the team to go on a winning
run. There was light relief from the grind of League Two football when
the second-tier pacesetters Wigan Athletic were beaten 1-0 in the Carling
Cup, widely agreed to be one of Grimsby's best attacking displays for several years. But in the league there were precious few signs that a truly concerted promotion bid could be launched. In the mayhem of the early
weeks, when the league table is all but meaningless, Grimsby veered as
high as seventh and as low as 21st, but once things had settled down they
occupied, for the most part, a place just below halfway.

And disappointingly, instead of getting slowly better as Slade and the other new faces got to know each other, results after Christmas 2004 slowly deteriorated. Too many games that might easily have produced three points were being drawn. The loss of the services of Dean Gordon and the talented but temperamental Ashley Sestanovich early in the New Year didn't help. The former would end up joining Apoel Nicosia of Cyprus, while the latter's absence from the team was largely due to issues of indiscipline. Sestanovich, on loan from Sheffield United, had only scored twice in 22 Grimsby appearances by the time he was sent off at home to Northampton after a display of petulance that saw Slade's patience finally run out, the player being sent back to Bramall Lane. This was merely the latest episode in a colourful career that would see Sestanovich appear as a 'double' for Thierry Henry in a Nike advertisement, and later convicted by a London court for his part in the planning of a robbery.

Slade needed more bodies in the second half of the season and, to add to the capture of Torquay's Martin Gritton, a regular from Christmas onwards, he signed Londoner Matt Harrold, a forward, on loan from Brentford. Harrold, twenty, scored on his debut shortly after half-time at Oxford, a goal which inspired a 2-1 win, and then bagged another to earn a point at Boston a week later.

It was a promising start, but proved to be something of a false dawn as Harrold never found the net again and Grimsby duly ended the season chalking up just one win from their final ten games – and even that was against already demoted Kidderminster Harriers. It meant the Mariners slid to a finishing position of eighteenth, well clear of departing Kidderminster and Cambridge United at the bottom, but also a very long way behind the promoted clubs Yeovil, neighbours Scunthorpe, Swansea and Southend.

It was a season that would not linger long in the memory, although notable for the fact that for the first time four Lincolnshire area clubs were in the same division – Lincoln, Scunthorpe, Boston and Grimsby – which meant a high number of derby games. Sadly for Grimsby, none of these six games ended in victory. By the end of 2004-05 the jury was still out on Russell Slade, indeed many fans were on his back and it was clear that if he kept his job for another season he would need to carry out more major surgery on the squad.

And, inevitably, the manager would have to do this once again on very limited resources. During the spring of 2005 the financial situation at the club became serious enough to prompt the chairman and then the Supporters Trust to issue public SOS appeals. The Trust announced:

'Grimsby Town currently have a major financial problem – for a club of their size and status – which threatens to force the club into administration. The Inland Revenue requires £720,000 in outstanding tax debts to be paid in the next three years if the club is to avoid a winding up order. The Inland Revenue accepts that this tax debt was in no way caused by financial mismanagement but by the collapse of ITV Digital and its subsequent consequences. At the time . . . the club was playing old Division 1 football and was therefore paying large sums on long contracts to most of the squad. Due to the limited size of Grimsby's fan base, the collapse caused major problems and, after maintaining Division 1 status for one year, the club was inevitably relegated, being unable to compete financially.'

Meanwhile, chairman Fenty had launched a 'Keep The Mariners Afloat' campaign, which the fans' trust had backed, pinpointing a figure of £120,000 they would raise for it. In all, the campaign was aiming for £420,000 to keep the club going, with planned initiatives including the non-matchday use of Blundell Park facilities. While certain clubs had been accused recently of going into administration as the 'easy option', Grimsby were determined this route would only be taken as a last resort.

Match of the Season 2004-05

GRIMSBY 5 BURY 1   League Two, 14 August 2004

With just one point from the opening two games under new boss Russell Slade, much-changed Grimsby welcomed unbeaten, no-nonsense Bury to Blundell Park. On paper it wasn't a fixture to stir the blood, but the 4,277 faithful were nevertheless in for something of a treat. Prior to the game, loanee forward Ashley Sestanovich had warned that Town's new forward line was beginning to blend well and he had a sneaky feeling they were now ready to take somebody's defence apart. How right he would prove to be.

Under a bright August sun, things failed to get underway in distinguished fashion, however. With the home fans taking their first look at veteran full-back Dean Gordon, newly signed on a week-to-week contract, barely 60 seconds had ticked by when the visitors won themselves a throw-in. Over strolled long-throw expert Dave Challinor, roundly jeered every time he touched the ball by those locals who remembered his hostile tackle of two years previously which ended the career of Grimsby's borrowed forward Martin Pringle. Challinor, undaunted by the barracking, hurled his missile into the danger area and home defenders seemed mesmerised as the ball evaded everybody to hit the far post. It bounced dangerously and was flicked up against the bar before falling to Brian Barry-Murphy, who drove home with his left foot to give the Shakers the lead.

It took Grimsby fifteen minutes or so to get themselves back on terms, an unmarked Darren Mansaram slotting in from twelve yards after Sestanovich did well to retain possession and thread the ball to him under considerable pressure. The scores remained level until the break, during which time Slade evidently found the right words to inspire his troops to produce a transformed second-half display.

Less than two minutes after the restart the anti-hero Challinor conceded a penalty, crudely challenging Andy Parkinson as Grimsby poured forward. Parkinson took one of those risky short run-ups and saw his kick clawed away by Garner. But from the resultant corner-kick the ball struck Challinor's arm meaning another penalty was signalled. This time Sestanovich stepped forward, only to see his less-than-powerful effort also blocked by Garner, but the rebound fell invitingly and the big loanee was first on the scene to knock in his first Grimsby goal.

The comfort of a two-goal cushion was achieved just after the hour when Thomas Pinault netted another rebound after a fine Parkinson chip from long distance had struck the underside of the bar and bounced out. The Frenchman was having a fine match and his first goal in Grimsby colours was rapturously received, to be followed shortly afterwards by a second, when he converted a pull-back by sub Michael Reddy, who was causing chaos on the flank. The Pontoon end went crazy and hailed their new French hero as he celebrated enthusiastically in front of them: Vive le Tommy!

Bury were by now very much a spent force and Town made it 5-1 when Jason Crowe fed Reddy, who swayed away from the attentions of demoralised defenders and turned to shoot home a fine goal. It was a rare treat for home fans to see their boys, particularly the likes of Sestanovich, flicking the ball around and turning on the show-boating. Pinault received a rapturous ovation when he was subbed, and the general mood was better than this ground had experienced for many a long month.

Chapter 5

A Season of Improvement
Ends in Disarray

Coca-Cola Football League   2005-06
Division Two (level 4)   4th (Play-off runners-up)
FA Cup   1st Round
League Cup   3rd Round
Football League Trophy   1st Round

It was to be another summer of major change at Blundell Park in 2005, with around a dozen players departing and the same number arriving, as manager Russell Slade strove to create a squad of genuine substance following the previous season's disappointments.

Among the fresh faces was a familiar one – old favourite Gary Croft, the talented local product who had left the club for a seven-figure sum nine years earlier but had under-achieved somewhat on his travels ever since. As a two-footed player capable of lining up in defence or midfield, Croft, now 31, looked the ideal type of player to add depth and quality to the squad. He was keen to kick-start a career interrupted by off-field problems. During a stint at Ipswich, Croft had become the first professional footballer to play a league game while wearing an electronic security tag. This dubious claim to fame followed his early release from prison where he had been serving a short sentence for driving while disqualified, and perverting the course of justice. He had to wear the device on his ankle for three weeks, and obey a night-time curfew. Croft later suffered injury problems which curtailed his appearances at Ipswich and then at Cardiff City, but was now eager to help his home-town club again.

Tranmere's long-serving striker Gary Jones was also among those recruited, despite advances by Welsh club Rhyl, who were not only nearer home but could offer the 30-year-old the chance of European football following their inclusion in the qualifying rounds of the UEFA Cup.

A mixed bag of results in the opening games, including a lacklustre home defeat by Darlington, saw Slade make major surgery to the side for a Carling Cup-tie at the home of Championship side Derby. He gave Jones his full debut, and also introduced centre-back Justin Whittle, a cult hero at neighbours Hull City, who had been controversially released by Tigers manager Peter Taylor. African-born central midfielder Jean-Paul

Kamudimba Kalala also made his debut after a successful trial period since arriving from Nice in France. The changes did the trick and Phil Brown's men were beaten by an early goal, Jones collecting a throw-in and turning to fire home. Kalala had a fine match and it turned into a night that saw things really start coming together for the Mariners.

Barnet and then Rushden & Diamonds were beaten over the August bank holiday weekend and Grimsby found themselves in the top six. Away form was particularly impressive, for in addition to the Derby triumph, Town managed to chalk up maximum points in each of their opening four games away from Blundell Park. Bristol Rovers, Barnet, Chester and Peterborough were the victims and, by the time of a mid-September home win over Torquay, Slade had steered the side to the very top of the League Two table. Sadly, only 4,026 turned up to see Town go top by beating the Devon side 3-0, but this figure was more than doubled three days later when Martin Jol bought his all-star Tottenham side to Blundell Park in the second round of the Carling Cup. This would really test the mettle of the new League Two top-dogs.

For Grimsby's new young midfielder Gary Cohen, this was a particularly big night, for he'd been born in London and was a lifelong Spurs fan. Having previously only played outside the Football League, Cohen was starting only the fourth senior game of his career and couldn't have picked more special opponents. The occasion would subsequently unfold as one of the great nights at Blundell Park, not just for Cohen, but for all attached to the club. Appropriately it was the anniversary of the club's formation (127 years earlier) and a near full-house crowd of over 8,000 cranked up the atmosphere and helped make Tottenham look highly uncomfortable.

England's Paul Robinson was the busier of the goalkeepers once the game had settled down and Grimsby snuffed out the early thrustings of their skilled opposition. Twice Robinson kept out Parkinson efforts and used his experience to force Reddy to narrowly miss out. England prospect Aaron Lennon caused problems with his speed down the flank, but there were few clear-cut chances carved out by Spurs. Stalwart full-back John McDermott was playing his 700th game for the home side and his energy and commitment overshadowed the contributions of several of the household names in the opposition ranks.

The tie remained deadlocked until the closing moments, the clock showing 88 minutes and extra-time looming when Grimsby's great moment arrived. Visiting substitute Sean Davis, who had replaced the subdued international Michael Carrick, headed clear a Paul Bolland corner. The ball fell for Kalala, stalking the edge of the penalty box, and he connected perfectly with a right-foot volley to send a raking drive into the net, a slight deflection off Michael Brown possibly hampering Robinson. The ground exploded and manager Slade set off down the touchline to celebrate in manic Barry Fry fashion.

Spurs had precious little time to respond to this body-blow, but a late effort by Robbie Keane went close, keeper Steve Mildenhall saving to loud cheers. Grimsby survived a nervous three minutes of stoppage time before Mr Laws' final whistle signalled a joyful pitch invasion. Man of the match Rob Jones was hoisted shoulder high by the fans. Even chairman Fenty was spotted down there among the Pontoonites celebrating at pitch level, and later footage of the scenes inside the home dressing room showed Fenty again at the centre of the action, leaping up and down ecstatically. During this sequence, Slade was called forward for an interview on camera, but promptly had a bucket of water poured down the back of his neck. Martin Jol admitted the defeat was probably the worst moment of his career as a club manager in England, and his centre-back Ledley King apologised for letting down the 1,500 Spurs fans who had trekked north for the game.

The Mariners were now on a roll, and a week later hammered previous leaders Notts County 4-0 in the league (Kalala bagged his fifth goal in only ten games) and maintained their fine away form by picking up draws at Boston and Shrewsbury, and a 3-0 win at Cheltenham. This stretched the unbeaten run on their travels to ten games overall. The Carling Cup's third round paired the Mariners with Graeme Souness's Newcastle, and the prospect of Alan Shearer and Michael Owen struggling to cope at Blundell Park attracted the cameras of Sky TV to provide live coverage to the world. For TV viewers, at least, the game would be best remembered for an incident involving Shearer and Town's uncompromising centre-half Whittle. An elbow belonging to the latter came into firm contact with the England legend's face, which, it was suggested, was an act of revenge for an earlier blow landed by Shearer. Whatever the history, the incident infuriated blood-spattered Shearer who spent the next few minutes berating the referee for missing it. Stitches at half-time stemmed the blood, but Shearer's annoyance remained highly visible for the rest of the game. Ten minutes from time Michael Chopra set up Shearer to drive home what would prove to be the game's only goal. Even this failed to placate the scarred striker, who refused to shake Whittle's hand at the end, leading to a scuffle and bad-tempered closing scenes.

From early November to mid-January a sequence of seven wins and three defeats from ten league games (21 points) ensured Town remained at or near the top of the division, and a genuine promotion challenge was materialising for the first time in nearly ten years. The stats around this period threw up some real anomalies, for by the start of 2006, Grimsby's home record for the season featured nine home defeats in the league (six losses) and cups (three), but away from home they'd only gone down once in fourteen matches. This perverse pattern would change dramatically after mid-January, however, for home form improved, with only one loss in ten, while only one away win was achieved in eight attempts.

Five new signings by Slade in January helped the side remain in contention throughout the run-in to May. A top-three placing was required for automatic promotion and Grimsby looked well set. Carlisle were the most consistent side around now and would ultimately lift the title, but Slade and his men were very much in the mix. A major blow en route to a thrilling finish to the campaign came in the shape of a humiliating thrashing by local rivals Lincoln, who were coming up on the rails late in the chase for play-off places.

A direct Imps side, fond of performing aerial bombardments, pounded Grimsby into submission on a day to forget for the 2,500 away fans who travelled down the A46. Two goals were conceded in the opening twenty minutes, the second a neat lob by former Grimsby favourite Jamie Forrester. Keeper Mildenhall then conceded a penalty and more woeful defending allowed a fourth Lincoln goal just before the interval. Slade was so furious at the inept first-half display that he conducted his half-time team talk in the centre-circle, in full view of the bumper 7,182 crowd. A tactics board was brought out from the dressing room and assistant Graham Rodger dutifully stood by, turning the pages of the flip-chart as Slade fingered exactly where they had all gone wrong. Perhaps this episode influenced Hull boss Phil Brown's decision to do something similar several years later when his side collapsed at Manchester City in a high-profile Premiership game?

Slade said it had been the worst 45-minute display in his time at Grimsby and felt his players didn't deserve to sit down in a comfy dressing room with tea and oranges: 'They embarrassed me, so I embarrassed them,' he said. His public dressing-down worked to a certain extent, for the flow of goals was stemmed for 40 minutes until the closing stages, when Croft lost possession and the Imps bagged a fifth. To make matters worse, it was reported after the game that around 170 fans from Grimsby had gone on the rampage in Lincoln in the worst example of football hooliganism in the area for many years. Three pubs were trashed, a set of gates at Sincil Bank were stormed and CS gas was used by police to quell the mob.

Grimsby had collapsed like a pack of cards in the face of Lincoln's physical approach and there were real fears the promotion bid would go the same way. Twelve points from the final seven matches of the season would probably be enough to secure automatic promotion, but that was easier said than done following such a demoralising setback. Grimsby overcame Wrexham 2-0 in the following game, but could win only one of their next five, scrapping for a 1-0 success at Cheltenham. It meant the difference between going up to League One automatically, or taking part in the play-offs, would be decided on the very last day with Grimsby relying on a result elsewhere to help them.

As the tension built in that final week, club officials were distracted by the announcement that legal action against Grimsby and one of its former players had been settled out of court. Former Scunthorpe player Peter Morrison reportedly won £400,000 damages following a tackle by Grimsby's Ben Chapman in a 2001 reserve game at Glanford Park. Morrison suffered a compound fracture of the leg in the incident, which saw Chapman red-carded and the game abandoned. Morrison underwent six operations in a bid to save his career, but in 2002 called it a day and began his legal action jointly against Chapman and Grimsby Town.

Grimsby's task on the final day of the season against already promoted Northampton at Blundell Park was to better Leyton Orient's result against relegation-threatened Oxford United at the Kassam Stadium. Orient were one point above Grimsby but had an inferior goal-difference. If Orient drew, Grimsby would need to win, but if Orient lost, the Mariners only needed a draw. The prospects for both matches looked favourable, for Northampton would surely be only cruising, having already secured promotion – while Orient would be up against an Oxford side desperate for points to try and stave off demotion to the Conference and urged on by a big crowd.

Northampton's visit generated a great atmosphere inside the ground, ticker-tape and balloons adding to the ubiquitous inflatable Harry Haddocks being waved in the air. Grimsby took the game to the Cobblers and were unlucky not to take an early lead, but all looked to be going according to plan when the breakthrough finally came on 75 minutes. Sean Dyche hauled down Gary Jones and Kamudimba Kalala stepped up to net the penalty amid scenes of huge tension. At this point the scores at Oxford were level at 2-2, so if things remained unchanged Grimsby were up. For more than fifteen minutes the status quo was nervously maintained, but Grimsby hearts went into mouths when the Cobblers won a corner with 93 minutes on the clock. Justin Whittle apparently believed he'd heard the final whistle at this point and momentarily began celebrating before realising his error. The flag-kick was whipped into the danger area and Dyche glanced it on. A mad scramble ensued and Ryan Gilligan got the final touch to equalise. Slade looked as if he was going into meltdown on the touchline, but most Grimsby fans were simply stunned into silence. Down at the Kassam, only a last-gasp winner for Oxford could send Grimsby up now. There was indeed a late goal in that match, but it went to Leyton Orient, who grabbed a last-minute winner. For Grimsby, the play-offs it was to be.

The two-legged semi-final pitted Grimsby against neighbours Lincoln again, but there was to be no repeat of the 0-5 hammering suffered by the Mariners on their last visit. Keith Alexander's hard-working side were stunned as Gary Jones struck for Grimsby on 22 minutes after good work from Andy Parkinson and Curtis Woodhouse set him up eight yards from goal. Lincoln desperately sought to get on terms and had two goals disallowed, for pushing and for offside, within minutes of each other. Town held on grimly and also survived an injury-time scare when Gareth McAuley hit their bar.

In the home leg three days later, Grimsby were the better side early on but fell behind midway through the first half, shortly after Imps striker Marvin Robinson and Town defender Rob Jones had suffered a nasty clash of heads. Robinson recovered, but Jones took no further part. Before substitute Ben Futcher could come on to replace him, however, Robinson got on the end of a free-kick and stooped to head Lincoln level on aggregate. On the hour came Grimsby's pivotal moment, a well-worked corner routine seeing the ball fired into the middle, where it was neatly turned in by lanky ex-Lincoln man Futcher. Having earlier been taunted with chants of 'Judas' by travelling Imps fans, Futcher celebrated brazenly in front of them.

With nine minutes remaining Grimsby made sure of an appearance in the final at the Millennium Stadium in Cardiff after Croft was brought down in full flight down the right. A pin-point Woodhouse free-kick was headed in by Gary Jones for his seventeenth success of the season. Near the finish Jones was sent off by Mike Dean for leading with his elbow in a challenge with McAuley, an offence likely to put him out of the big day in Cardiff. The final whistle sparked delirious scenes, a pitch invasion followed by a curtain-call in the Main Stand of Grimsby players to acknowledge their delighted fans. It was fourth time unlucky for the nearly-men of Lincoln in the League Two play-offs.

For Grimsby there was much more action still to come in 2005-06, both on and off the field. The play-off final (see 'Match of the Season' below) would be followed by a crisis behind the scenes as negotiations broke down concerning the renewal of Russell Slade's expiring two-year contract. Stalemate was reached and on Wednesday, 31 May Slade quit Blundell Park altogether, with the rumour-mill indicating that Yeovil Town were waiting in the wings to offer him a job. The League One out-fit wanted an experienced man to replace Steve Thompson, who was reverting to coaching after nine months at the helm at Huish Park. Within a few days Slade was indeed confirmed as Yeovil's new manager. Back in Grimsby, chairman John Fenty ended the speculation about his replace-ment by handing the task to assistant Graham Rodger, the loyal 39-year-old Scot who had previous experience as caretaker.

As well as losing Slade, the man who had masterminded the promo-tion chase, Grimsby also said farewell to important players such as Mildenhall, Woodhouse, Kalala and player of the season Rob Jones, who was sold for £250,000 to Hibernian. The latter's sale, plus the proceeds of the Carling Cup run and play-off final, helped appease HM Revenue & Customs, who were owed a considerable sum, but Grimsby fans were inevitably left feeling that a decent side was now breaking apart and that years of struggle might be on the horizon again. They felt the newly introduced management team of Graham Rodger and assistant Stuart Watkiss was chosen by the board of directors as a cheap option, and even though finances appeared to have been somewhat stabilised, there didn't seem to be much optimism on the terraces.

Match of the Season 2005-06

CHELTENHAM 1 GRIMSBY 0   Play-off final (Cardiff), 28 May 2006

In the build-up to the play-off final at the Millennium Stadium, Grimsby and Gary Jones were able to persuade the football authorities that the lat-ter's use of his elbow against Lincoln had not been malicious and his automatic suspension was cancelled. The team could now face John Ward and his Cheltenham side, an outfit they had beaten twice in the league, at or near full-strength. The Harry Haddocks and replica shirts were every-where as 15,000 headed to south Wales, desperate for a repeat of the play-off win at Wembley against Northampton eight years earlier.

The final competitive 90 minutes of the entire 2005-06 campaign was played before almost 30,000 spectators at the end of May, with promo-tion to League One the prize. An uneven pitch made things a little tricky but both clubs had coped with much worse, and it was the west country side who went closest in the opening stages. Steven Gillespie and Steve Guinan both appeared to lack composure when good chances presented themselves. Both sides suffered a setback when a clash of heads between Michael Reddy and the Robins' Craig Armstrong saw both players removed with suspected concussion. It was a crushing blow for Grimsby in particular, for this was the type of stage seen as ideal for Reddy's flamboyant skills, but he'd been knocked out cold and the physio recommended he should not continue. More bad luck followed when the industrious Andy Parkinson was clearly brought down by Gavin Caines but referee Paul Taylor brushed aside penalty claims.

There was sheer disbelief in the Grimsby camp at this, but the players recovered and Cohen and Parkinson went close to scoring before the break. After half-time the game turned into a dull, deadlocked affair until the 63rd minute when Grimsby's third stroke of bad luck proved decisive. Steve Guinan took possession on Grimsby's left and from the edge of the penalty box attempted a cross towards substitute Kayode Odejayi. The ball eluded everyone and somehow curled in low at the far post to give the Robins the lead and bring the match to life. Guinan would later admit his effort had not been intended as an attempt on goal.

Cheltenham then won a penalty after an illegal Woodhouse challenge, only for the victim, midfielder Grant McCann, to pick himself up and have his spot-kick saved by Mildenhall. The keeper had further saves to make in the later stages of the game and watched another effort from McCann come back off his crossbar. At the other end Gary Jones missed a great chance to equalise when his header was saved by Shane Higgs. It was not to be Grimsby's day and another season in the league basement beckoned. Russell Slade admitted that the underdogs, who had finished the season six points behind Grimsby, had been the better side over the 90 minutes, although he felt luck deserted his men as regards the non-penalty and the loss of key man Reddy.

Chapter 6

Rodger and Out

Coca-Cola Football League	2006-07
Division Two (level 4)	15th
FA Cup	1st Round
League Cup	1st Round
Football League Trophy	2nd Round

With Grimsby having gone so close to promotion in May 2006, Graham Rodger had to cope with high expectations when he began his first stint as the fully fledged manager of the club in the summer. He recruited the former Mansfield Town and Kidderminster manager Stuart Watkiss as his right-hand man, and four new players were quickly signed to replace the high-profile departures who had followed Russell Slade out of Blundell Park.

Fleet-footed forward Isiah Rankin, a 28-year-old Londoner, needed no introduction for he had had a twelve-game spell with Grimsby in 2004 when his four goals couldn't help stave off relegation during Nicky Law's reign as manager. Since then, Rankin had spent two seasons at Brentford. Big Scots defender Gary Harkins, formerly at Blackburn, also signed on the dotted line, along with goalkeeper Phil Barnes from Sheffield United, who had been understudy to Paddy Kenny. But the biggest surprise of all was the capture of 40-year-old winger Peter Beagrie, who had recently left neighbours Scunthorpe to concentrate on his media work at Sky Sports and ITV, but had been talked into talking a player-coach role at Blundell Park.

As well as joining the small, exclusive club of professionals who had played beyond their 40th birthday, Beagrie had recently chalked up 750 games and 100 goals in an itinerant 23-year career that had taken in Middlesbrough, Sheffield United, Stoke, Everton, Manchester City, Bradford City, Scunthorpe, plus loan spells at Sunderland and Wigan along the way. He acknowledged that playing at his age meant he was seen as 'a bit of a freak', but reckoned he was naturally fit and could go on longer – and even promised to uncork his trademark celebration somersault if and when he scored.

Things got off to a thrilling start in the opening match at home to Boston, with Grimsby coming back from a two-goal deficit with less than a quarter of the game remaining, to win 3-2. Two of the goals came from teenage debutant Peter Bore, a locally born substitute for Michael Reddy. He netted with his first touch in the 67th minute, later adding the winner after Rankin equalised. The delight was temporary, however, for Town failed to win any of their next seven league and cup games, and Rodger was forced into the transfer market to try and rectify matters.

By the end of October only five wins had been chalked up in nineteen matches in all competitions, one of those in a penalty shoot-out, and the Mariners had slumped gloomily into the bottom four. The only ray of hope during this period was a 2-1 win over Walsall, who were setting the pace at the top of the table under their new manager, Richard Money.

Experienced goalgetter Tony Thorpe, at 32 hanging on to the vestiges of a stop-start career, was captured on loan by Rodger in September and put straight into the side. He failed to score in five games and was not the answer to Grimsby's immediate woes. The anticipated promotion challenge had simply not materialised, and even the evergreen enthusiast Beagrie had second thoughts about his decision to prolong his playing career. With the Mariners sitting 89th in the Football League, his contract was duly cancelled by mutual consent and Beagrie announced his decision to retire from the game entirely during an appearance on one of Sky's sports shows.

A miserable 1-3 defeat at home to promotion-challengers MK Dons in front of the lowest gate for eighteen months saw the Blundell Park crisis deepen in the first week of November. Grimsby only had two shots on target all game and, after the visitors bagged their third goal on 79 minutes, home fans left the ground in droves. Many of those who remained began chanting for the removal of the manager and even a late consolation goal, and a firework display in the distant sky, failed to lighten the mood. Two days later, apparently with heavy hearts, the chairman asked Graham Rodger to step down, publicly praising his loyalty and dedication, but saying the Scot had become a cruel victim of circumstances. Stuart Watkiss took temporary charge of a squad of players said to be highly upset at what had happened to Rodger, who had served the club for fourteen years.

The board of directors acted not only quickly, but in a way that surprised many, when they replaced Rodger with 55-year-old Alan Buckley within a few days. Buckley was returning for a third stint as manager at Blundell Park in a period that spanned eighteen years. He still lived locally and had been out of the game full-time since leaving Rochdale in late 2003, but having guided Grimsby to a promotion and Football League Trophy double in 1998, he had the approval of many fans. He announced that he was up for the challenge and reckoned he had 'some unfinished business here', referring to his unhappy departure in 2000. He was also at pains to point out that he had mellowed since his last incumbency: 'I'm not the hothead I once was,' he quipped.

The new era got underway with a couple of creditable away draws, at Paul Lambert's promotion-chasing Wycombe in the league, and at League One side Northampton in the FA Cup. But this new feelgood factor at Blundell Park receded somewhat when the replay with the Cobblers ended in a 0-2 home defeat in front of a low crowd. However, Buckley had an ace or two up his sleeve in the shape of some useful loan signings. A huge impact was made by the energetic forward Martin Paterson, borrowed from Stoke, who would go on to hit four goals in the next three league games. Paterson, later a star name at Burnley, was introduced into the side alongside fellow loanees Anthony Pulis (the Stoke midfielder, son of their manager Tony) and Peter Till (Birmingham winger). The tide had turned it seemed, for Buckley could boast a proud record of four wins and a draw from his first half-dozen league games since returning. Following a 2-0 home win over Torquay, the Mariners occupied the heady heights of sixteenth in the table, and Christmas 2006 arrived with relegation worries beginning to fade.

Long-serving full-back and skipper John McDermott chose this period to quietly announce he would be quitting after the end of the current season. His astonishing tally was 21 seasons and a club record number of first-team appearances. The 37-year-old, who hailed from Middlesbrough spent his entire career at Blundell Park and had by now exceeded 750 games and was truly part of the furniture. He was one of fewer than twenty players in the history of English football to play more than 600 Football League matches for a single club. His first-team debut came at Bradford City in February 1987, the week of his eighteenth birthday, and he went on to win the club's Player of the Year award a record three times, the BBC Radio Humberside Sports Personality of the Year award, and promotion or relegation no fewer than nine times. His remarkable appearance tally would have been even higher but for serious injury in 1994 which kept him out for nine months. No wonder there would later be a campaign – so far unfulfilled – calling for McDermott to be awarded an MBE.

McDermott's exit would certainly mark the end of an era, and thoughts of change were also brought to bear when the local council granted outline planning permission for Grimsby Town's new stadium project on the edge of the neighbouring village of Great Coates. This was a significant step forward in a process that had been underway for more than twelve years.

A report to identify the best site for relocation of the Mariners had been commissioned back in 1994, but it was five years before the paperwork was submitted identifying the Great Coates A180 interchange site as the only suitable place for the new ground. As is usually the way with such projects, there was a mountain of red tape to be negotiated. By 2002 the matter had gone before a planning inquiry, which delved into the suitability of the site following objections from local residents. Around this time the giant oil company Conoco were unveiled as the official sponsor, whose name the new stadium would carry. Another year then went by before the region's 'Local Plan' was formally adopted with the Great Coates football ground project included. By early 2006 a planning application for a 20,000-seater stadium had been submitted, and now permission to move ahead was finally on the table. Excited noises about clearing out of Blundell Park by the year 2009 were made, but in view of the speed of progress thus far, this seemed a tad optimistic. The more immediate problem was surely improving results to ensure that Grimsby didn't kick off in their new home – whenever that might be – having lost their Football League status.

It may have been nothing more than coincidence, but the significant progress concerning the move to a new ground seemed to signal an end to the Alan Buckley 'honeymoon period'. Following his good start, Grimsby slipped up at Hartlepool on Boxing Day and this sparked a losing run that would stretch to seven miserable games, only a single goal being scored in the entire period, and that was in the seventh losing game, a meaningless late consolation after conceding four at basement club Torquay. A crop of injuries contributed to the slump, which inevitably plummeted the team back into the league's nether regions. They found themselves even worse off than Lincolnshire neighbours Boston, who had gone into administration.

At the end of January 2007, with 30 games played, Grimsby were in a perilous position – just one point clear of the trap door, but with the two clubs below them both having games in hand and much better goal-differences. One of this pair was Rochdale, who had recently appointed Keith Hill as manager, and were just embarking on what would prove to be a remarkable revival, ultimately shooting them from 23rd up to ninth in a matter of just three months.

In case the fans hadn't noticed, the local press made much ado about this fast turning into the club's worst season for nearly 40 years. But supporters who felt Buckley had failed and should have been sacked already were warned that in the 1968-69 campaign the Mariners finished 91st in the Football League after changing managers twice during the season.

Few can seriously have expected Buckley to be ousted so soon after his reappointment, but, on the other hand, even those willing to be patient with him could never have anticipated the dramatic turnaround in fortunes that was around the corner.

That grim run of successive losses was abruptly halted with a thumping 6-0 success away to Boston that had stunned supporters reaching for their record books (see 'Match of the Season' below). In the wake of this Boston glee party, the stay-away fans flocked back to Blundell Park – the attendance for the visit of Bristol Rovers a week later was almost double that of the previous home game with Darlington. Rovers were beaten in a 4-3 goal bonanza which started badly for Grimsby, conceding sloppy goals to fall 0-2 behind with a third of the match gone. The Mariners were only stung into action after loud claims for a penalty were turned down, and they proceeded to net four times in a glorious 33-minute passage of play that had the crowd roaring its delight. Rovers grabbed a late goal to bring it to 4-3, a scoreline that made the contest look closer than it had really been.

The two wins represented an astonishing about-turn after the recent run without goals or points, and lifted the team clear of the relegation zone. However, the poor defensive work which allowed Rovers to score three gave the Blundell Park pessimists the opportunity to cast a shadow over events. The diarist on the *Cod Almighty* website was in despair as he witnessed fans still moaning despite seeing a previously hapless team suddenly score ten times in three hours. He tried to find reasons for this bizarre attitude:

'Living in Grimsby means several things. On the positive side, it means a cheap mortgage and constant access to the greatest fish and chips on God's sweet Earth. But in the debit column it means rows upon rows of identical pebble-dashed houses with boxy white PVC bay windows, and it means hearing ill-informed conversations about these "asah-lum seekers teckin all aah jobs". Having one's roots on the south bank of the Humber also entails a hereditary optimism deficit, with the result that many of the 5,883 supporters who watched the Mariners' amazing 4-3 win over Bristol Rovers on Saturday will have gone away perversely convinced that [goalkeeper] Phil Barnes was directly to blame for the Gasheads' goals, that Alan Buckley should be sacked for signing Matty Bloomer, and probably that Danny Boshell is rubbish.'

But even this deep-rooted negativity slowly lifted as Grimsby followed their goal-sprees with another five victories in the next six matches – Ciaran Toner, Danny North and Paul Bolland getting themselves among the goals. Relegation worries were completely banished and for a few days in mid-March the club climbed briefly into the top half of the league table, something that had seemed impossible a few weeks earlier. A number of players starred in the final weeks of the season, notably younger players like Peter Bore, Danny North, Nick Hegarty and Ryan Bennett, the latter becoming the club's youngster ever skipper when donning the armband in a goalless draw with Lincoln. The roller-coaster ride that was the second half of Grimsby's season was encapsulated in microcosm in the closing weeks, when the team were well beaten 1-4 at lowly Accrington Stanley, only to bounce back seven days later with a 5-0 thrashing of recently improving Barnet. It was all very confusing, and certainly gave the local bookies a headache. The Mariners had become the League's most unpredictable outfit.

The campaign ended in front of a bumper crowd in celebratory mood at Shrewsbury's Gay Meadow in a match meaningless for Grimsby, but with the home side needing a point to make certain of a League Two play-off place. It was also the last scheduled league game at the 97-year-old stadium before the Shrews moved to a new home at the New Meadow Stadium. If Grimsby were to spoil the party and beat Gary Peters' men, not only would Shrewsbury miss the play-offs, they would have to say goodbye to their long-standing home today. For the Mariners contingent, however, most of their emotional energy was tied up with saying farewell to loyal defender John McDermott, playing his last game for the club after 22 years' record-breaking service.

Andy Taylor had the homesters chewing their nails when he gave Grimsby a first-half lead, punishing some defensive hesitancy, but the highly motivated Shrews drew level through a controversial Ben Davies penalty after the same player had tumbled when chasing a cross. Home celebrations were put on hold when Grimsby subbed McDermott, and play was interrupted as both sets of fans gave the retiring skipper a lengthy and rousing ovation.

Barely had the applause died down and the tears been dabbed away, when Shrewsbury central defender Kelvin Langmead headed home a Davies free-kick to make it 2-1. But it was the visitors who insisted on the last word, equalising in the very last minute of the season when Nick Fenton stabbed in from close range. It meant a nervous ending for the home side, who survived with a point to reach the play-offs on goal-difference from Stockport.

For Grimsby, a finishing position of fifteenth left them thirteen points adrift of a play-off place, but a comfortable 23 clear of demotion. It had been an odd season of ups and downs, during which they managed to beat five of the clubs who were promoted or made the play-offs. Only that appalling run of results immediately after Christmas spoiled what might otherwise have been regarded as a very positive campaign.

Match of the Season 2006-07

BOSTON 0 GRIMSBY 6   League Two, 3 February 2007

More than 1,000 Grimsby fans ventured the 50 miles south for this 'local derby' wondering when on earth their team's appalling run of form would be halted. Since Christmas, seven successive losses had been suffered and in the 630 minutes of action (not including stoppage time) that entailed, they'd only scored a single goal – and even that was a consolation effort which came at the very end of the seventh and most recent defeat. It was not just a bad run, it was verging on the catastrophic.

Perhaps loanee Martin Paterson's late strike at Torquay, the first Grimsby goal in over six weeks, served to lift the jinx that was bedevilling the Mariners' forward line. For by half-time at Boston they'd managed to smite no fewer than four goals without reply into Andy Marriott's net. Suddenly there was no holding the no-hopers.

The tone was set as early as the fourth minute, when young Peter Bore, starting a match for the first time since December, headed in a looping cross by Ciaran Toner. Three minutes later Bore went on a run and crossed for James Hunt to open his account for the Mariners to double the lead. The away fans were in dreamland and with just twenty minutes on the clock their favourites made it three, Toner turning smartly to rifle in from the edge of the box. Bore grabbed his second shortly before the interval, heading home a fine cross by Tom Newey. Stunned Boston were in complete disarray – they'd not expected this from the deflated team they'd recently overtaken in the league table.

On the hour, Paterson side-footed home a volley after Nick Fenton's header had hit the bar and rebounded his way. Paterson celebrated wildly with the jubilant cod-heads and was yellow-carded for his trouble. Twelve minutes before the end the sixth goal went in, Bore completing a hat-trick by drilling in Paterson's cross at the near post. The day was made complete for the fans when their side invited cries of 'ole' by cheekily keeping possession instead of trying to press forward. It only served to upset the bruised home egos even further. It was Grimsby's biggest away win in 50 years and meant they leapfrogged Wrexham, Macclesfield, Accrington and Boston, and escape from the dreaded lower regions.

Manager Buckley dedicated the victory to his chairman ('who has been working his socks off lately') and especially to the fans who had travelled the 640-miles round trip to Torquay a week earlier, only to witness an abysmal 1-4 defeat. Today had been one of those surreal games where the reasons for the unexpected outcome were hard to pinpoint. Nick Fenton and Justin Whittle were back together as central defensive partners and this made Grimsby look far stronger than of late, although Boston did nonetheless manage to hit the underside of the bar and have two efforts cleared off the goal-line. Generally though, the York Street side were dreadful and could have no complaints about their pasting.

There was worse to come for Boston. Losing their last game, at Wrexham, meant they finished next to bottom and were demoted to the Conference. They chose to have their ten-point deduction for various financial transgressions implemented this season rather than next, but they ended up automatically dropping two divisions instead.

Grimsby's Alan Pouton displays the art of the overhead kick at Anfield in October 2001. The central midfielder helped the Mariners to a shock 2-1 win in the Worthington Cup on a memorable night in front of a crowd of 32,672. Costing £150,000 from York City in 1999, the big Geordie Pouton would spend five years at Blundell Park, gaining huge popularity for his never-say-die attitude. Injury and suspensions kept his appearance tally down to 116 games and he bagged twelve goals. He joined Gillingham in 2004 for a five-figure fee and was still active in non-league football in 2010

Popular defender Ryan Bennett, who joined Grimsby in 2006 after being released as a young-ster by Ipswich Town. He made his Mariners debut as a late substitute shortly after his seven-teenth birthday, against MK Dons in April 2007. He went on to establish himself as one of the lower divisions' brightest prospects, making more than 100 appearances for Grimsby. Mike Newell made him captain while still a teenager, and, despite repeated overtures from Peterborough United, Bennett stayed at Blundell Park until shortly after Newell was sacked in October 2009. His final Grimsby game before joining Posh was the pivotal 0-2 home defeat by Rochdale which led to Newell's exit

Midfielder Andrew Wright (No.28) was recruited in 2010 on loan from Scunthorpe, to help the Mariners' bid to return to the Football League

Scots midfielder Peter Sweeney (right) in action at Blundell Park. The former Stoke and Millwall man joined the Mariners on loan from Leeds in March 2009 and later signed on a full-time basis. He made a total of 48 appearances and scored four goals, including a brilliant volley against his former club in a cup-tie at Elland Road. He was released after demotion in May 2010 and joined Bury

Liverpool's Gary McAllister attempts to block a Paul Groves pass during Grimsby's famous Worthington Cup win at Anfield in 2001. Derby-born Groves, a no-nonsense midfielder, first joined Grimsby in 1992 after spells with Leicester and Blackpool and hardly missed a match in four seasons, scoring consistently from midfield. He followed manger Alan Buckley to West Brom for a £600,000 fee in 1996, but a year later returned to Blundell Park. He was made captain and boosted his league appearance tally for the Mariners to well over 400 in this second spell. He was twice voted Player of the Year and played a key role in the successful 1998 'double' winning side. Less than three months after this appearance against Liverpool, Groves stepped up to become the club's player-manager after the departure of Lennie Lawrence. Groves steered the club clear of relegation in 2002 but subsequently lost his job in 2004. In more recent times he has had spells as Portsmouth's caretaker manager and landed a senior coaching role at West Ham under Avram Grant

Grimsby substitute Peter Bore is out-jumped by an MK Dons defender in the 2008 Johnstone's Paint Trophy final at Wembley, which the Buckinghamshire side won 2-0. Grimsby-born Bore burst on to the scene in 2006, scoring twice as an eighteen-year-old substitute on his debut, to inspire a 3-2 win over Boston after the Mariners had earlier been two goals behind. In the return match later that season Bore hit a hat-trick in a remarkable 6-0 triumph at the York Street ground. Originally a nippy winger, Bore was successfully converted into a right-back and won the Player of the Year award at the end of the ill-fated 2009-10 season, during which he passed the 100-appearance mark for the Mariners

Phil Jevons (No 21) celebrates his astonishing last-minute winner for Grimsby at Liverpool in the 2001 Worthington Cup. Jevons, then 22, had been signed a few weeks earlier for a substantial fee from nearby Everton, for whom he had made eight league appearances. His long-range goal in the dying seconds stunned Anfield and was witnessed by a large number of Jevons' family members and acquaintances from the local area. Jevons went on to make 63 league appearances for Town, scoring eighteen goals, leaving the club after relegation in 2004. He had a loan spell at Hull and later moved to Yeovil, Bristol City, Huddersfield and Morecambe

Goalkeeper Phil Barnes and defenders Nick Fenton and Robert Atkinson applaud the 25,000 Grimsby fans at Wembley, following the disappointing 0-2 defeat by MK Dons in the 2008 Johnstone's Paint Trophy final. After this anti-climax at the home of football, Town only won two of their remaining eleven league games and finished a miserable sixteenth in League Two. Even worse was to follow in the subsequent two seasons, of course

Striker Charles Adameno was one of the 2010 summer signings by manager Neil Woods as he rebuilt Grimsby's squad to face the challenges of its first season outside the Football League. The Milton Keynes-born target-man began his career at Southend United in 2007, making just four league appearances for the Essex club and being loaned out to five different non-league sides. He finally found his feet during the 2009-10 season with Crawley Town, for whom he scored eleven goals in 32 league games, including a sensational hat-trick inside eight minutes against Grays Athletic. Adameno made his Grimsby debut as a substitute against Hayes & Yeading in August 2010

Danny Carlton arrived at Blundell Park to help the Grimsby cause in September 2010, via a loan arrangement with Bury. The 26-year-old Leeds-born striker had earlier played for Carlisle and Darlington, but enjoyed his best football at Morecambe, where he notched 61 goals in 188 league games, in two separate spells at the Christie Way club

Talented French-born Jean-Louis Akpa Akpro was a free agent when he arrived at Blundell Park in December 2008, invited for a trial by manager Mike Newell. He had not been taken on by MK Dons nor Colchester after trials, but after an impressive outing in the Mariners' Reserves he signed a contract and made his first-team bow in the home win over Shrewsbury shortly afterwards. Having earlier appeared for his home-town club Toulouse and the Belgian side FC Brussels, Akpa Akpro was Newell's third signing of a French-speaker, the others being Jean-Paul Kamudimba Kalala and Mickael Buscher. Akpa Akpro was an enigmatic performer, his occasional flashes of brilliance including the occasion when Lincoln were thrashed 5-1 in March 2009. By the time that demotion from the League was assured, Akpa Akpro had totalled 56 league appearances for Town, scoring eight goals. He rejected the offer of a new contract and joined League One side Rochdale in July 2010

Around 25,000 Grimsby fans enjoyed a day out in the Wembley Stadium sunshine in March 2008, although the event ended in disappointment as well-drilled MK Dons lifted the Johnstone's Paint Trophy with a 2-0 win. Danny Boshell had a penalty saved by the Dons keeper before Paul Ince's men took the lead with their own, controversially awarded penalty, netted by skipper Keith Andrews. Sean O'Hanlon's powerful header sealed Grimsby's fate minutes later. It was Grimsby's third appearance at Wembley under manager Alan Buckley, and the fans were certainly not outsung, even if they were outnumbered and beaten. They club had won its way to Wembley thanks to wins over Huddersfield, Rotherham, Doncaster, Stockport and Morecambe. MK Dons went on to lift the League Two title later that season, while deflated Grimsby went on a run of eight successive defeats (including the final) ensuring their 2007-08 season ended with a whimper

Wolverhampton-born Dwayne Samuels pulled on the black-and-white stripes for the first time in serious competition when called up to face Hayes & Yeading in August 2010. Right-back Samuels, still only nineteen, had made his way through the youth ranks at West Bromwich Albion, but was released by Baggies boss Roberto di Matteo after they won promotion back to the Premier League in May 2010

Grimsby made a moderate start to life outside the Football League, winning six and losing five of their first fifteen Conference fixtures. Wins over well-fancied clubs like Luton, Crawley and Newport were countered by defeats at the hands of Hayes & Yeading, Tamworth and Fleetwood. Average home gates of just over 3,000 witnessed eleven goals in the first eight home matches up to mid-October, including the one pictured here, being celebrated by Peter Bore (No 2), Danny Carlton (No 18) and Andrew Wright (No 28)

Danny North shields the ball, surrounded by Cheltenham players in a match that ended goal-less in January 2010 at Blundell Park. It was the eighteenth successive match in league and FA Cup in which Town failed to register a victory

Michael Coulson in attacking mode against Lincoln in February 2010. The game finished 2-2

The curse of the programme cover! The editors chose veteran Irish goalkeeper Nick Colgan as cover star for the visit of Crewe to Blundell Park in August 2009, but it was loanee Tommy Forecast who got the nod to play between the sticks following an injury to Colgan. The former Hibs, Barnsley, Ipswich and Sunderland keeper subsequently won his place back and went on to make 35 league appearances during 2009-10

Grimsby's Peter Bore takes to the air against Darlington at Blundell Park in September 2009. This was Bore's first start in 2009-10, but ended in disappointment when he was substituted and Town could only draw 1-1 with the Quakers, thus failing to build on the victories chalked up in the previous two games

Well-travelled Lee Peacock hit the net for Grimsby in this stormy home game with Lincoln City in February 2010. It was his fourth appearance for the Mariners since joining from Swindon and he registered his first goals for the club, one in each half. The 33-year-old Scotsman Peacock (now at his seventh club) had debuted three weeks earlier alongside fellow newcomers Dean Sinclair and Tommy Wright. Manager Neil Woods had high hopes of this trio but their contribution to the fight for survival was ultimately all in vain

Defender Paul Linwood gets stuck into this challenge with former Grimsby favourite Phil Jevons of Morecambe in March 2010. The 1-1 draw at the Globe Arena would be the last time the former Chester City skipper Linwood started a match for Town. After 28 appearances and one goal during the demotion season, he was released and joined Fleetwood Town

Mark Hudson in midfield action during the 1-1 draw at Morecambe in March 2010, in which Town came back from a goal down to earn a precious point. Hudson played for Middlesbrough, Chesterfield, Huddersfield and Rotherham, had arrived from Gainsborough Trinity on trial, one of a number of new faces recruited to help the survival fight. He notched two goals in eleven full appearances, and remained on the club's books for the start of the non-league era

After a stormy but largely successful stint as manager of Luton Town, Mike Newell was invited to take the hot seat at Grimsby in the autumn of 2008, following the sacking of Alan Buckley. A year later, with the club still in the League Two doldrums, a row behind the scenes precipitated Newell's departure. He achieved promotions as manager of Hartlepool and Luton, but success at Blundell Park eluded him and he could only inspire thirteen wins from a total of 53 games in charge of the Mariners

Jean-Louis Akpa Akpro gives Darlington defenders something to worry about during a 2-0 win in April 2010

Robert Atkinson cracks home a beauty to set Grimsby on the road to a 2-0 win against relegation rivals Barnet in the penultimate match of 2009-10. The win set up a dramatic last day

Forward Nathan Jarman featured on the cover of the match programme for the 2009 FA Cup-tie with Bath City, a humiliating home defeat reckoned by many to represent a new low point in Grimsby's recent decline. After 46 league appearances in three years, Jarman left Blundell Park in May 2010, his final season featuring trouble reportedly sparked by messages of discontent he posted on the social networking site *Facebook*.

Robert Atkinson (No 25) has put Grimsby ahead in the home game with Darlington in September 2009, and is congratulated by Peter Bore (left) and Danny North. The Quakers later equalised and Town had to be satisfied with a point, meaning their mini-revival after a bad start had stalled. This would be the first game in a sequence of 25 league matches without victory

Big striker Tommy Wright seen in action in the crucial home game with Barnet in May 2010, for which he was recalled to the starting line up after an absence of four games. The 25-year-old arrived from Aberdeen in January 2010, but failed to win over many Town fans, largely due to his lack of goal output (just one in fourteen games). In August 2008 he had cost the Dons a substantial fee from Darlington, to whom he returned after quitting Grimsby in the summer of 2010

Town's Danny North shields the ball on the flank during the September 2009 win at Torquay. The 2-0 triumph took the Mariners out of the bottom four for the first time in many months, but the joy was short-lived for a marathon winless run stretching to 25 games followed this Plainmoor encounter. For their part, Paul Buckle's Torquay were also embarking on a season of struggle, but eventually recovered to steer themselves well clear of the relegation trap door

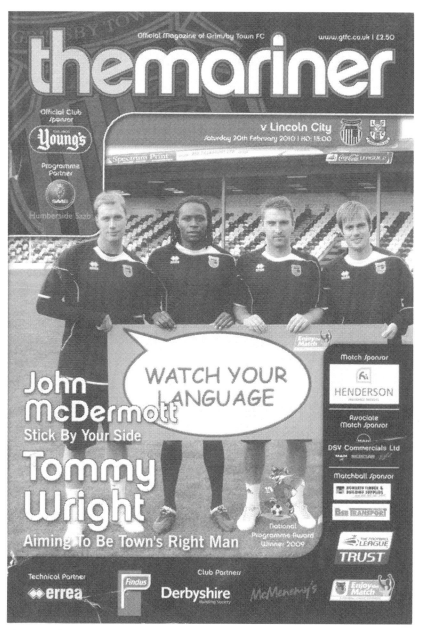

The matchday programme for the 2-2 derby game with Lincoln City in March 2010, one of four drawn games during that month. The programme cover publicised a 'Watch Your Language' campaign, which was largely unsuccessful thanks to the anger among Grimsby fans when the match officials made controversial second-half decisions that denied Town victory. Lee Peacock bagged both Town goals, either side of the interval, in the entertaining 2-2 draw

Jean-Louis Akpa Akpro takes possession during the 2-0 win at Torquay in September 2009. After five games out of the squad, Mike Newell recalled the Frenchman for this game and he was introduced as a substitute for Chris Jones. An own-goal by the Gulls' Kevin Nicholson and a strike from Peter Sweeney gave Town the three points at Plainmoor

Joe Widdowson brings the ball under control against visitors Rotherham in August 2009. The left-back proved one of the team's most consistent performers during the horrendous 2009-10 season, making 38 league appearances. Adam Le Fondre's penalty opened the scoring for the Millers in this match, but Peter Sweeney equalised, only for Michael Cummins to bag what would prove to be the the winner shortly afterwards. It condemned Grimsby to their fourth defeat in the opening four games of 2009-10 season, with twelve goals conceded and just two scored. This bad start set the tone for a campaign of almost unrelenting misery

Michael Coulson (No 21) provided some of the better moments of a bad season after he arrived at Blundell Park in November 2009 on loan from Barnsley. Coulson made his name at his home-town club Scarborough before moving to Oakwell in 2006. Here his progress was hampered by a serious knee injury and he was allowed to try his luck at Grimsby following loan spells with Northwich Victoria and Chester City. Coulson would bag five goals for misfiring Grimsby in 2009-10 and is seen here bursting down the flank in the tense final-day encounter at Burton Albion in May 2010

They may be out of the Football League after 99 years, but there is still interest in Grimsby from the TV companies. The match with Luton Town in September 2010 attracted live TV coverage and saw all the trucks and equipment pitching up behind the Findus Stand – just like the old days!

The matchday programme for the vital home game with Torquay in April 2010, which ended in a horrendous 0-3 defeat, a result which boosted the Gulls' survival chances and proved a near-fatal blow to the home club's prospects. Cover star was Nick Hegarty, one of the few employees to have been at Grimsby throughout the decline in the club's fortunes between 2001 and 2010, the era charted by this book. Hegarty signed in 2001 on a youth scholarship deal, made his debut in 2005 and would make 92 league appearances before becoming one of seven men released after demotion hit the club in 2010. In the summer he moved to Scotland to join St. Mirren

Olly Lancashire (left), Robert Atkinson and Lee Peacock (No 37) put the Darlington defence under pressure in Town's 2-0 away victory of April 2010

Lee Peacock (left) is about to scramble the ball home to register Grimsby's opening goal in the 2-2 home draw with neighbours Lincoln in February 2010

Grimbarian Danny North prepares to cross the ball during the 1-2 home defeat by Rotherham in August 2009. North was a local product who made his first team debut in 2004 aged just seventeen, during Russell Slade's stint as manager. When he netted against Burnley in August 2007, North had the honour of claiming Grimsby's 7,000th goal in all competitions. North would make a total of 81 league appearances for the club, scoring seventeen goals, before falling out of favour during the Mike Newell era, and finally departing in February 2010. He has since turned out for Scunthorpe, Alfreton and Irish club St Patrick's Athletic

Michael Coulson struggles to gain possession during the goalless draw with Cheltenham on a bitterly cold January day in 2010. Town's long run without a win went on and this was also the twelfth game of the season so far in which they failed to score. Town stood 23rd in the League Two table, with their visitors just two places higher

Michael Coulson tries to weave his way around two Morecambe defenders at the Globe Arena in March 2010. The contest ended all-square thanks to the goal scored by Coulson on the hour, which cancelled out the first-half strike by the home side's Paul Mullin. With Morecambe still harbouring play-off hopes, this was seen as a valuable point for the Mariners, who were attempting to stage a late-season revival and avoid the drop

Lee Peacock makes a nuisance of himself in the final match of the 2009-10 season at Burton Albion's Pirelli Stadium. To avoid relegation Town needed to win this game and hope Barnet failed to beat Rochdale at Underhill on the same afternoon. Both outcomes failed to materialise, Grimsby slumping 0-3 and Barnet winning 1-0. For Paul Peschisolido's Burton side, the result marked the end of a satisfactory first season in the Football League, in which they established themselves safely in mid-table

Danny North attempts to retain possession under pressure from a Darlington defender during the 1-1 draw at Blundell Park in September 2010. The point earned, thanks to Robert Atkinson's first-half goal, left the Mariners in seventeenth place and hopeful of continuing their rise away from the bottom of the league – a dream that ultimately proved unattainable

Lee Peacock goes sprawling under the challenge of a Barnet defender in the tense penultimate game of the 2009-10 season at Blundell Park. Peacock had come on as a substitute for Tommy Wright and used all his experience to help Town hang on to the lead given them on the hour by Robert Atkinson. The pressure was released in the final minute when Mark Hudson made it 2-0, to the delight of a 7,000-plus crowd

Demotion after 99 years as a Football League club. Will the last man out of Blundell Park please turn off the lights?

The Findus Stand is an imposing edifice at Blundell Park, viewed from the car park outside (above) and from the visitors' seating (below). Visiting supporters from other Conference clubs will doubtless be impressed by the superior facilities on offer

Chapter 7

A Huge Anti-Climax

Coca-Cola Football League	2007-08
League Two (level 4)	16th
FA Cup	2nd Round
League Cup	1st Round
Football League Trophy	Beaten finalists

Manager Alan Buckley made all the usual optimistic noises at the start of the new season, but there were few new signings of note, and several well-known names had departed. With John McDermott now retired and Michael Reddy's career wrecked by a long-standing hip injury, it looked highly debatable whether the squad was strong enough to improve on last season's finishing position in the lower half of the table. But Buckley was a man of experience and know-how and he seemed convinced the dressing room contained enough talent and depth to take the club forward, following the surge to safety in the latter half of 2006-07.

Teenage defender Ryan Bennett led the early charge, scoring soon after the start of the season's opener at home to Notts County, but that impetus was not maintained and the first four league and cup games of the season all frustratingly ended all square at 1-1. An impressive 4-1 win over Huddersfield Town in the Johnstone Paints Trophy came as a relief, although it only disguised the poor progress in the league, and defeats at Shrewsbury and Accrington Stanley meant Grimsby were in the all-too-familiar position of 23rd in the table by early September. Drawing at home to Stockport next time out, meant the Mariners had failed to win any of their six opening league fixtures.

Playing well in patches, Grimsby looked far too good to be serious relegation candidates, but glaring defensive lapses and a lack of punch in attack was undermining all the hard work. Buckley juggled the team and changed tactics on a number of occasions to try and smarten things up, but when his defensive formation for away games was employed for home fixtures too, his critics made their views known. Victories by 2-1 over Lincoln and Hereford saw September end on a happier note, but it would prove only a brief respite from the gloom.

Ironically, Grimsby never failed to score in any of the first twelve league and cup games of the season. Nevertheless, the main issue was the lack of goals from the strikers, with even the arrival of new signing

Martin Butler from Walsall in October failing to solve the immediate problems. Between them, Isiah Rankin, Danny North, Gary Jones and Butler – the men whose main task was to get the ball in the net – failed to score a single goal in the opening sixteen league games. At this point midfielder Paul Bolland found himself the club's leading marksman with just three strikes.

Butler, a lively 33-year-old Midlander, came to Blundell Park on a three-month loan arrangement (later signing permanently) to pep things up, but it wasn't until a November FA Cup win over Carlisle that he was able to help the smiles return to Grimsby faces. After a 1-1 draw in Cumbria, the replay with the League One leaders attracted only 2,008 into Blundell Park, but they saw an exquisite winning goal, thrashed home by Gary Jones, thus breaking his scoring duck for the season. Town also struck the post twice and managed to keep a clean sheet for the first time this season in 22 attempts. Carlisle, with John Ward newly installed as manager, were at this stage 45 league places better off than Grimsby, and the confidence generated by beating them helped Buckley's injury and ill-ness-hit side chalk up a handsome 3-0 win at Barnet the following Saturday.

By now, the progress in the FA Cup had been matched by that in the Johnstone Paints competition, where the Mariners had reached the northern semi-finals, the victory over Huddersfield having been followed by draws and penalty shoot-out wins over Rotherham and Doncaster Rovers. Having only gone out of the Carling Cup on penalties (at home to Burnley), Grimsby had by now remained unbeaten in normal play in six cup-ties. However, gaining just three wins in seventeen league games was a far more relevant statistic, and it pointed to another fight against relegation being on the cards.

The momentum generated by the big win at Barnet evaporated after the onset of December, the side going down at Huddersfield in the FA Cup and then suffering a 0-4 pasting at home to Darlington in the league. The latter outcome was the type of horrendous result that often prompts dark mutterings about a manager's future. Such talk was rife among impa-tient fans and in the local media, but it was clear that Buckley's job was being made much harder by the injuries and illnesses affecting his first-choice line-up. The chairman was probably not seriously thinking of a change of manager at this point, for his hands seemed full dealing with the fall-out from the new stadium project. A budget shortfall had appar-ently been identified, and John Fenty also had to deny suggestions from disillusioned fans that the whole Great Coates venture was really just a plan designed to make him rich.

The fourth goal conceded in the massacre by promotion-chasing Darlington was a real comedy of errors, but as the newcomers began to settle in their new surroundings, loanee defenders Rob Atkinson and Sam Hird looked capable of tightening things up at the back. A few more clean sheets and Grimsby would surely be back in business. Sure enough, the luck that had generally been deserting them in league matches turned Grimsby's way for their trip to west London, where they snatched a 1-0 win at Brentford despite being completely outplayed for much of the game.

This was followed by another single-goal triumph, albeit over bottom-of-the-table Mansfield, but the points kept Town chugging along just above the bottom four. They were scratchy wins, but they kick-started the sort of proper revival that some fans must have despaired of ever seeing this season.

After Christmas the atmosphere at Blundell Park was transformed as the side embarked on a ten-match unbeaten run in the league (winning seven) and made their way to the northern final of the Johnstone Paints Trophy. It propelled Grimsby into mid-table and coincided with Atkinson, Hird and Nick Hegarty, back from a loan spell at York, becoming settled in the side, Gary Jones getting his starting place back in attack, and fellow forward Danny North having more luck in front of goal. A shocking 1-4 home loss to Dagenham & Redbridge saw the team momentarily knocked off course, but four-goal wins over Barnet and Morecambe saw them bounce back nicely, and at one point Grimsby even reached the heady heights of ninth in the table.

This was a far cry from the pre-Christmas gloom, but a serious play-off challenge was never really on the cards. A 2-1 win at doomed Mansfield in March left Grimsby five points adrift of Darlington, who were in the final play-off position (seventh), but eighth-placed Rochdale had three games in hand on Grimsby. It would need a phenomenal late charge to get any higher in the table. As it would turn out, rising into the top half of the table prompted a bout of altitude sickness, and Grimsby contrived to lose all their remaining seven league games, slipping back down to sixteenth in the process.

At least part of the reason for the late slump, of course, was the distraction of an epic run in the Johnstone Paints Trophy. Stockport were beaten in the northern semi-final away, and a Paul Bolland goal snatched a 1-0 triumph in the northern final first leg at Morecambe. Grimsby only needed a draw in the second leg at home to reach Wembley and the highest gate of the season, 7,417, arrived at Blundell Park in party mood. Confidence was sky-high following a 4-0 league victory over the same opposition, on home ground, just three days earlier. Grimsby looked such hot favourites to reach Wembley that it was all a little worrying – and the third meeting of the clubs in eight days did indeed prove no easy ride, ending goalless.

It meant Bolland's first-leg goal at Christie Park was decisive, and Grimsby were back at Wembley again under Alan Buckley, ten years after he guided the team to the memorable 'double' of 1998. The opposition at the newly refurbished national stadium would be League Two's champions-elect MK Dons, or the 'franchise scum' as more outspoken Grimsby fans preferred to call them (one of the supporters groups produced T-shirts bearing the slogan 'Franchise football: Never forgive, never forget', and donated half the profits to the supporters trust at AFC Wimbledon).

The cup final (see 'Match of the Season' below) and the period that followed would spark a massive anti-climax to this up-and-down campaign. One of the worst finishes to a season in living memory for Grimsby fans would see the last seven league games all end in defeat, and any outside chances of a play-off place quickly vanished into thin air. Grimsby had come away from Wembley knowing that if they produced a better finish to the season than Chesterfield and Rochdale, they might sneak into seventh place. It was only a glimmer of hope, and it rested on the Mariners winning at least five of their final six league games, and their rivals faring worse than that.

Unfortunately, Grimsby's remaining opponents were all in the top ten and Town lost to the lot of them. Rochdale picked up 21 points from their final games to show how it was done, and it was they who reached the play-offs. The writing was on the wall for Grimsby less than a week after the cup final when they lost 1-3 at Rochdale, and after that the season simply petered out as the club slipped down to sixteenth, one place lower than the previous year.

It had been a strange season, not without occasional high spots, but ultimately one of disappointment again. The league tables rarely lie, and they showed it was highly questionable whether Grimsby Town had made any satisfactory progress at all in the past few years. By the end of 2007-08 the Mariners seemed as far as ever from escaping up from the league's basement division.

The new stadium saga was rolling slowly onwards in the background, and it was even suggested the Mariners could be playing there by 2011, but the prospect of League Two football (or worse) in a new 20,000-capacity home in front of just 3,000 souls wasn't a particularly exciting one.

Match of the Season 2007-08

GRIMSBY 0 MK DONS 2   JPT final, Wembley, 30 March 2008

Paul Ince's promotion-chasing side from the Buckinghamshire metropolis had led the League Two table since September and went into this game in superb form, unbeaten in their last eleven league games (winning seven). Grimsby, for their part, were in much better shape than earlier in the campaign, but their confidence and consistency was not on a par with their opponents and they started the final very much the underdogs.

The Mariners chances were hardly helped six days before the final, when they had a 'pre-Wembley wobble' at home to Brentford, losing 1-2, having led at half-time. Alan Buckley was not amused and kept the players locked in the Blundell Park dressing room for about an hour afterwards. Their second-half display had been well below par and seriously damaged the outside hopes of reaching the play-offs. Buckley's anger implied that the players had taken their feet off the pedal a little, to save themselves for the big day at Wembley.

Twenty-five thousand tickets were sold for the Grimsby sections at Wembley and there was the familiar build-up to the big day, with the media highlighting tales of exiled fans flying in from far-flung locations for the game. One example was the 38-year-old IT specialist Michael Oakes, who was determined to be at the match even though his itinerary involved catching a plane from the Cayman Islands to Miami, then another to New York, then another to the UK, and finally a train to Cleethorpes before heading to north London. The team bus had a less convoluted task to get to Wembley and headed for the capital on the Friday lunchtime, in preparation for a Sunday lunch-time kick-off.

Many fans were not prepared to risk leaving their travel to the last minute, and set off in a southerly direction more than 24 hours in advance. More than 1,000 of them headed directly for Trafalgar Square for a photo-call organised by the *Grimsby Telegraph*. To the bafflement of foreign tourists in the area, this event took place in pouring rain and there, right in the middle of the damp but happy melee, was none other than club chairman John Fenty. As all life-long supporters of an unglamorous club know only too well, red-letter days such as these come along all too infrequently, and need to be enjoyed to the full. Once the rain stopped, and it was revealed that injured top scorer Danny North had declared himself fit to play, all seemed well with the world. Nevertheless, realists knew that MK Dons had done the league double over Grimsby, and their 1-0 win at Blundell Park came just three weeks before the final.

A healthy 56,618 attended the game, joined by millions more, thanks to live Sky TV coverage, and they witnessed a contest in which Grimsby's luck was definitely out as regards two key incidents, but the final was deservedly won by MK Dons. The statistics told the tale, with Ince's men registering twenty goal attempts and striking the woodwork, while Grimsby mustered just five.

There was early hope for the noisy Mariners contingent when North got clean through on goal, but he was unable to maintain composure and scuffed his shot. Several minutes later there was more drama in the MK goalmouth as flamboyant goalkeeper Willy Gueret brought down Paul Bolland, but got up to save Danny Boshell's penalty-kick. The Dons looked a well-drilled outfit and after these early scares took a grip of the game.

Soon after the break, Keith Andrews motored through for a clear sight of goal but lost his one-on-one with Grimsby keeper Phil Barnes. The stalemate was finally broken on 74 minutes when Nick Hegarty was harshly adjudged to have pushed the Dons' Danny Swailes, and the penalty was tucked away by Andrews. Many Grimsby folk noticed that an assistant's offside flag had been raised a split-second before the alleged push, but referee Phil Joslin was unmoved by the Grimsby protests. The trophy was put beyond the Mariners' reach six minutes later when Sean O'Hanlon headed in from a Colin Cameron corner, his effort skidding off Rob Atkinson's head before hitting the net.

The two penalty outcomes had killed Grimsby, but manager Buckley was honest enough to admit that the better side on the day had won. MK Dons would go on to top the league table too, thus emulating Grimsby's feat – ten years earlier – of winning promotion and the Football League Trophy in the same season. One minor consolation was stressed by an emotional chairman Fenty, who reckoned Grimsby's 25,000 fans had completely out-sung their 30,000 counterparts and had left him 'humbled' by their level of support.

As a footnote, it was interesting to note that not every Grimsby fan able to travel chose Wembley as their destination over this weekend. One of the diarists on the *Cod Almighty* website explained: 'A few of us went to watch AFC Wimbledon, to present them . . . with the profits from the ['anti-franchise football'] T-shirt sales. And we had a magnificent time, only marred by the Wombles' most unfortunate 2-4 loss. The atmosphere was tremendous, the bar had proper beer and the reception we got was very touching. Believe me they were all rooting for [Grimsby against MK Dons at Wembley] and we got some nice messages of commiseration afterwards by email.'

Chapter 8

Newell and Renewal

Coca-Cola Football League	2008-09
League Two (level 4)	22nd
FA Cup	1st Round
League Cup	2nd Round
Football League Trophy	2nd Round

The previous summer may have been relatively quiet at Blundell Park, but during the 2008 close season manager Buckley decided the Mariners' squad must undergo major surgery if the decline of recent years was to be halted.

He recruited three defenders and a midfielder, each with lengthy experience in the lower divisions, also borrowed a hungry young ball-winner from Barnsley, and threw all five of the new faces into the League Two fray for the opening game. However, he was unable to find anyone to boost the potency of the forward line, and Grimsby's lack of goalpower would soon become a major issue.

Defeated play-off finalists Rochdale were in town for the opening game of the new season, and Grimsby's quintet of debutants included three in defence – Robbie Stockdale, Richard Hope and Matt Heywood, the latter given the skipper's armband. Twenty-nine-year old Stockdale had been snapped up after being released by Tranmere and was a full Scotland international with five caps, who had begun his career at Middlesbrough. Alongside him was tall stopper Hope, a 30-year-old who arrived from Wrexham, freshly relegated to the Conference. He had well over 300 league games to his credit, including a long spell at Northampton. Heywood, meanwhile, was a wholehearted player possessed of leadership qualities, who arrived from Brentford where he'd recently been voted the Bees' fans player of the year.

In midfield, Mariners fans were introduced to Welsh international Chris Llewellyn, another capture from Wrexham, who had started out at Norwich, for whom he played nearly 150 games in seven years. Promising Barnsley youngster Simon Heslop, only one league game to his name, was also put straight into the Grimsby side following the bad news that Paul Bolland would be missing for several months with a serious knee problem. Also out of the reckoning was veteran striker Gary Jones, quitting for family and injury reasons, and about to try his luck at non-league club management in Wales. The other absent friend was defender Nick Fenton, a regular for the previous two years, who was allowed to join Rotherham on the eve of the big kick-off in August.

The changes showed that Buckley certainly wasn't resting on his laurels, but they didn't seem to generate much excitement from the down-to-earth Town supporters, some of whom scoffed when chairman John Fenty gave defiantly optimistic interviews about the club's immediate prospects. Fenty said if ever there was a season where Grimsby had a good opportunity to succeed, this must be it, citing the disappearance from League Two of the promoted richer clubs like Peterborough and MK Dons, and the huge points deductions meted out to rivals Luton Town, Rotherham and Bournemouth. Luton would kick off the season on minus 30 points, with Rotherham and Bournemouth on minus seventeen. Clearly, if any two of those clubs overhauled Grimsby to send the Mariners down, performances must have been bad indeed. Nevertheless, Fenty said he understood fans' concerns and called for them to be patient while the new-look team gelled.

In addition to worrying about the on-field prospects, Fenty was fighting another battle over the new stadium project. It was feared the Great Coates plan might be severely hampered by local councillors giving the go-ahead for a £30 million retail park elsewhere in the area; it was felt this new plan would prove more attractive to big-name retail stores than would the football stadium's associated retail space.

With unsettled Martin Butler, injured Danny North and inexperienced youngsters Andy Taylor and Nathan Jarman the only striking options, Grimsby's pre-season workouts failed to generate much optimism, and, perhaps predictably, the opening league game with Rochdale ended goalless.

Three days later fewer than 2,000 turned up to see Tranmere defeated 2-0 in the Carling Cup, a result which showed Buckley had something to work with, but any confidence generated that evening was knocked sideways by a 0-4 hammering at Brentford the following Saturday. The Bees came good after being let off the hook early on, thanks to glaring misses by Butler and Taylor.

Defeat by Brentford meant the club had to say goodbye to one of the few smiling faces currently to be found around Blundell Park just now. The author and TV producer Spencer Austin had devoted the past few weeks of his life entirely to Grimsby Town. He was embarking on a project he had devised called 'I Am the Gloryhunter'. It involved him putting 92 numbers in a hat, drawing one out and moving to live in that town, immersing himself in local life and following their football team until they lost a game. Then he would move on to accompany the club that had beaten them, and so on, throughout the season. His adventures were being filmed for ITV and would be recorded in book form at the season's end. The lucky dip to find his starting point had seen Grimsby Town pulled out of the hat.

Most Grimsby fans that Austin had encountered found the whole thing hilarious and warned Austin that supporting the Mariners until they lost a match would mean his attachment to this great fishing port would be a very short one. For his part, Austin threw himself enthusiastically into the task of becoming a Grimbarian and the publicity he received ensured plenty of attention at the club's first two games of the season. Club officials even presented him with a replica shirt so that he could dress appropriately. 'There's only one gloryhunter,' chanted the Pontoon-standers during the Rochdale game, many of them apparently pleased to have this unexpected distraction from the struggles of the team out there on the pitch.

Positioned in the midst of the Grimsby fans who travelled down to Brentford to see their favourites fall three goals behind by half-time, Austin filmed events and recorded his thoughts: 'The mood goes from away-day celebration to abject doom within just 45 minutes. Brentford tonk Grimsby so profoundly that I expect some of this lot will need treatment for post-traumatic stress disorder; the players will only be identifiable by dental records. They'll be enduring harrowing flashbacks for years to come. It's brutal. With the final whistle comes the first evidence that this glory-hunting game is for bastards. All my burgeoning relationships and half-plans to explore Grimsby some more come to a smacking halt.'

A week later, the general air of depression that Austin wrote about deepened when Chesterfield left Blundell Park with a 1-0 win. It was a game completely without atmosphere, thanks partly to the noon kick-off and partly to the growing conviction among home fans that if their side avoided relegation this season it would probably only be thanks to the points deductions suffered by three other clubs.

A few days later there was fleeting excitement when full-back Tom Newey gave Grimsby an unlikely early lead in the Carling Cup third round tie at Premiership Blackburn. Paul Ince's men (Ince's success at MK Dons had seen him snapped up by the Premiership outfit, but he would not last long), soon settled and hit back with four goals to win comfortably. Grimsby followed this defeat by scrapping for a point at Lincoln City, but there was more disappointment on the cards when transfer deadline day came and went with no sign of the new striker that the fans so desperately craved. Only young Manchester City full-back Javan Vidal was added to the injury-hit squad, on a loan deal.

Inevitably home attendances were dropping game by game, and fewer than 3,000 attended the September meeting with Chester City, who were eighteenth, just two places above Grimsby at the time. A forgettable first half saw Chester take the lead, but after sub Danny North levelled soon after the interval, Grimsby showed a lot more purpose than of late and applied pressure in the search for a winner. The visitors rode their luck, keeper John Danby making several superb saves, before two fine strikes late on by veteran striker Kevin Ellison finished Grimsby off. A missed penalty by Danny Boshell in the dying moments only added to the air of gloom.

In the match programme that afternoon, the chairman had insisted that the club's board was 'committed to stability' – but less than 48 hours after referee Mark Haywood blew the final whistle on the 1-3 defeat, Alan Buckley was sacked. His third and shortest stint as the club's manager came to an inglorious close. He had been sacrificed just one game short of being in charge of the Mariners for 600 games in all. Some fans questioned the timing of the board's decision, but it was clear something had to be done, for Grimsby had by now failed to win a league game in six months (thirteen matches) and were twentieth in the table (three of the four below them having started with massive points deficits).

Fifty-seven-year-old Buckley had first become a Football League manager 29 years and three months earlier, in the summer of 1979, and, in all, had been in charge of five different clubs for well over 1,000 games. His total of ten years in office at Blundell Park had produced many highs and lows, and at least he could claim the club had never been relegated under his watch.

The club's official statement said they had acted because of the run of poor results, and within an hour or two of their Monday morning revelations local bookmakers Don Noble were quoting assistant manager Stuart Watkiss as hot favourite to take over. It was the sixth time in only four years that a new manager was being sought. Buckley, a touchline orgy of noise and remonstration during matches, had showed plenty of commitment to his task, but had been severely hampered by budgetary limitations.

Watkiss took the role of caretaker-manager for the second time since his arrival in 2006. He quickly introduced young Ipswich midfielder Liam Trotter on loan and marshalled the troops for a trip to the opposite coast of northern England, where the team claimed their third point of the season in a 1-1 draw at Morecambe. Idle thoughts surfaced that this might be the start of a turnaround in fortune in advance of lowly Barnet visiting Blundell Park a week later. For the north Londoners were stumbling along in even worse form than Grimsby – they had drawn once and lost six of their seven league matches thus far. Bearing that in mind, plus the fact that Watkiss had found another two young loanees to boost the Grimsby attack, there was at least some cause for hope, surely?

Barnet only brought 81 travelling fans with them, but some of the recently absent Mariners supporters returned to witness the first home match since the close of the Buckley era. They were to be horribly disappointed by the most dire of contests. The visitors looked inept, disjointed and struggled to put passes together, but sadly Grimsby seemed at a loss over how to punish them. New boy Tomi Ameobi, borrowed from Doncaster and the younger brother of Newcastle's Shola, had an ineffective debut, as did Malvin Kamara, a London-born Sierra Leone international midfielder, loaned from Huddersfield. The latter at least had the excuse that he had been unable to carry out his usual pre-match ritual, which apparently involved watching the film *Willy Wonka and the Chocolate Factory*, a procedure that normally calmed him and prepared him for action.

Barnet took the lead with a scrappy goal, completely in keeping with the tenor of the game, Albert Adomah's cross bundled past keeper Phil Barnes by midfielder Neil Bishop. Early in the second period, Watkiss lost patience with his misfiring side and made a triple substitution, bringing off Hunt, Ameobi and Llewellyn, but ultimately to little effect. It would be seven minutes from the end before the Mariners' first genuine effort on target arrived. By then, some fans had given up the ghost altogether and left, while others were chanting derogatory songs at their own team. The final whistle came as blessed relief from this torture, with Barnet's loyal band of 81 celebrating as if they'd won promotion, and home fans shaking their heads in disbelief. Things, as they say, could only get better.

In the wake of this horror show it was revealed there was a shortlist of eight for the vacant manager's job, some of whom did not apply for the position, but had been head-hunted by the board. The way the team was performing, it was clear the sooner a new man came in to get a grip of things the better. The Barnet debacle was followed by a 1-4 humbling at Rotherham (all four conceded in a 31-minute spell). This result helped to confirm that the home side's seventeen-point deduction would not necessarily condemn the Millers to the lower reaches of the table for the entire season. Sharp-eyed observers keen to spot Grimsby's managerial candidates reported that the game was watched from the stands by Mike

Newell, Martin Foyle, Mick Wadsworth and the Liberian national team manager Antoine Hey. This quartet – four very different people in terms of personality, experience and background – were understood to have been interviewed by the Grimsby board in the days before the Rotherham game. The successful candidate would be unveiled within 48 hours, announced the chairman.

When the big moment came, it was former Hartlepool and Luton Town boss Mike Newell who got the nod. The 43-year-old Liverpudlian's appointment was a surprise in some quarters, for when the vacancy had first arisen Newell featured as low as No 13 on the local bookies' top twenty contenders. Anyone who took a punt back then would now be celebrating. It was a brave choice by John Fenty, for Newell had gained a reputation in football as a feisty character, not slow to challenge authority and make himself unpopular if he felt the need. He had a history of major spats with the people who employed him at both his previous clubs. Grimsby were about to discover whether or not Newell's eighteen-month sabbatical from the game had seen him mellow.

Grimsby were one of only two senior clubs in England without a victory at this point, and it was hardly the type of job Newell had once seemed destined for. While enjoying success at Luton three years earlier, Newell had been courted by a number of Championship clubs. The idea of him taking over a demoralised outfit near the foot of League Two had then seemed highly improbable – but three years is a long time in football management. Newell's public outbursts on controversial subjects such as female officials, football's so-called bung culture, and the capability of the hierarchy at Luton Town, had seen him sacked at Kenilworth Road in March 2007, and he'd been in the footballing wilderness for the eighteen months since. He was nowadays regarded at best as 'high maintenance', or at worst as somebody not be touched with the proverbial barge-pole. But his CV featured two promotions in less than five years of management and players apparently liked him, if administrators did not. The appointment won early approval from the canny fellows at the *Cod Almighty* website, a group whose opinions could normally be relied upon as well considered: 'Newell is a genuinely exciting appointment which ought to unite the fans and galvanise the players,' wrote their diarist.

Newell's colourful managerial record tended to overshadow his considerable accomplishments as a player. A hard-working striker, he had played for thirteen clubs in nineteen years, scoring well over 100 goals in around 500 games. He starred in the top division for the likes of Luton, Everton and Blackburn, where he forged a fine partnership with Alan Shearer. At Ewood Park he was remembered for scoring 'the perfect hat-trick' in a European Champions League tie – three goals in only nine minutes against Rosenborg – with his left foot, right foot and head.

Newell said he was excited by the potential at Grimsby, and not overly worried by their lowly league position: 'I watched them on Saturday at Rotherham and for a team in the position they're in I was pleasantly surprised.' He said the most important factor in taking the job was that Grimsby had wanted him and taken the trouble to call him. He added that it had taken over a year to recapture his passion for football after what happened to him at Luton. His largely successful reign had been blighted by ending miserably with a run of 28 games featuring only four wins. The axe had fallen reportedly due to 'gross misconduct' after he publicly criticised the way the club was being run at board level, among other things.

Newell added that opportunities had come along for him to return to football during his exile from the game, and he'd even turned down the chance to become an agent – a move that would have been a classic case of gamekeeper-turned-poacher. It was clear, and he virtually admitted as much, that he had become something of an outcast after his Luton experiences, and that some people now viewed him as an outspoken trouble-maker.

According to the *Daily Telegraph,* had Grimsby not offered this route back into football management, Newell may well have ended up in another form of employment. Grimsby's idea to approach Newell had only come along several days after Buckley had been booted out, when chief executive Ian Fleming heard Newell on a BBC Radio 4 show discussing illegal payments in football, and explaining how he had helped 'blow the whistle' on this problem, thus sparking an official inquiry into it. Mr Fleming apparently liked the cut of the Newell jib, and Grimsby went and got their man. He took official occupation of the hot-seat for the first time on the Tuesday morning after a Johnstone Paints Trophy 1-2 defeat at Scunthorpe. According to details that would enter the public domain some time later, Newell's basic starting salary was £1,265 per week and he also stood to gain five per cent of profits from outgoing player transfers. His contract ran until the end of the following May (2009), and would only be renewed if the club avoided relegation to the Conference. Given the whopping points deductions handicapping Luton, Rotherham and Bournemouth, surely Grimsby were not worried about the spectre of relegation? The contract clause proves they clearly were.

Newell's first game in charge came the following weekend at home to Wycombe Wanderers, when admission prices were reduced to encourage locals to come and witness the start of the new era. The crowd exceeded

4,500 for the first time in eight games and they were up on their feet in the first minute when Peter Bore made sure Nick Hegarty's shot crossed the line after barely 40 seconds of action, to give Newell the perfect start. However, keeping Wycombe at bay for the remaining 89 minutes proved a daunting task, even when the visitors were reduced to ten men by a sending off. With stoppage time looming, the resistance was finally broken and Leon Johnson headed an equaliser and the long run without a league win continued. A week later, another battling performance, this time at Exeter City, was rewarded with a point from a goalless draw. It was only two points from a possible six, but at least there were signs that Newell had stopped the rot.

Newell didn't make radical team changes immediately, but the atmosphere at Blundell Park seemed to be improving. However, the lack of a victory in his two opening games created some unwelcome club records which perhaps deflated things a little. Failing to beat Wycombe in the tenth league match of the season meant this was now officially Grimsby's worst ever start to a season (four draws and six defeats). Then, the draw at Exeter meant the winless run going back to March had been extended to eighteen league matches, equalling the all-time club record, set when George Kerr managed the side some 27 years earlier.

Next up for Newell was a midweek visit of his former club Luton, one of just three clubs (artificially) below Grimsby in the table. Fun and games were assured, if only due to the fact that Newell had left Luton under a cloud, and was taking legal action against them for wrongful dismissal. Certainly, the 200 or so Hatters fans who made the Tuesday trip north seemed to be in light-hearted mood and very keen to exchange 'banter' with their former boss. Their behaviour was no doubt enlivened by the presence of a writer and photographer from men's magazine *loaded*, who accompanied them, curious to discover the attraction of a midweek trip to Grimsby to watch two struggling teams from League Two (with a combined points total of minus thirteen).

The embedded journalists travelled to Blundell Park in a Lutonian mini-bus and were astonished by the optimism and fervour they witnessed on the road into Grimsby: 'Man's ability to party as his world goes tits up is legendary and that's ultimately what makes us better humans than women. During the Russian Revolution, the incumbent Tsar greeted the end by drinking heavily and snorting the coca leaf. Some 30 years later, as the Russians rounded on Berlin, the Nazis – who are not to be admired of course, but prove a point nonetheless – danced, made love, drank and snorted Lord Charles. When Scarface knew his chips were well and truly up, he buried his craggy Cuban boat into a mound of snoot shortly before raining bullets. The mandrill monkey faces certain death by expending every last second of life in the pelvic thrusts of sweet, sweet love. Following Luton Town to Grimsby on a Tuesday night during a season of inevitable relegation to a non-league status is a similarly noble death dance.'

Peter Bore, the local lad whose two years of ups and downs in the Grimsby first team had qualified him for the over-used football adjective 'enigmatic', once again surprised his critics by scoring in the very first minute, lashing home after his first attempt was blocked on the goal-line. It temporarily demoralised Luton, who were on a run of five games without a win. But from the dugout, Newell's former deputy Mick Harford rallied his black-and-orange clad troops and before long they were level after Tom Craddock was hauled down in the area. Minutes later, Grimsby survived appeals for a second spot-kick when Craddock was again flattened. It had turned into a poor first-half display by the Mariners after that great start, but things improved vastly after the break. Ryan Bennett headed home a Peter Till cross just before the hour and the prospect of a first league win in seven months (thirteen defeats, five draws and no victories) loomed large. But the nervousness as this milestone got closer seemed to spread from crowd to players and back again, the seconds ticking slowly by. For more than half an hour the 2-1 lead was held, but in the 92nd minute resistance crumbled and another couple of points went west. And just to make matter worse, the dirty deed was set up by a slip of a boy who was only playing thanks to his headmaster letting him off lessons that day.

Jordan Patrick, at sixteen years and seven days, became the youngest player in Luton's 123-year history when he came off the bench in those final few moments. Due to an injury crisis, Luton had been granted permission to whisk him away from Challney High School for Boys to make the trip to Grimsby, and now he was about to make his mark. Deep into stoppage time he took possession, slipped a clever through ball to Craddock and the equaliser was drilled home. Cue pandemonium in the Osmond Stand, silence and depression elsewhere. Nineteen league games without victory was a new Grimsby club record.

Mike Newell pondered how on earth he could conjure up a winning performance from a group of players who had simply forgotten what victory tasted like, while his beleaguered chairman considered the growing disquiet over the club's new stadium project. The local council had reportedly suggested that a different location might now be worth considering. Since the Great Coates plans were first drawn up, the football club's finances had become much less healthy and the economic viability of out-of-town retail outlets to accompany the stadium had been seriously eroded.

Newell had suffered a bellyful of new stadium red tape while at Luton, and wisely focused his mind on finding a winning formula on the field. The 2-2 draw against the Hatters was followed by two defeats and seven goals shipped to Bradford City and Dagenham & Redbridge, the month of October ending with Town on a measly six points from fourteen games. Without the points docked from Luton, Bournemouth and Rotherham, Grimsby would have been four points adrift at the foot of the Football League. There was no hiding from the fact that things had rarely, if ever, looked this bad before.

Newell dived into the loan market to recruit former Grimsby players Jean-Paul Kamudimba Kalala and Robert Atkinson. Their second debuts, at home to Darlington, didn't have a happy ending, even though both played well. The horror show of recent weeks continued in the early stages, with the Quakers going 2-0 up in the first fifteen minutes. Well before half-time Town's much-criticised centre-back Matt Heywood was withdrawn from the fray, which at the time looked like a Newell response to nightmare defending, but which the club later stated was due to a thigh injury. Could things get any worse?

In fact, from this point, things did improve slightly. Atkinson replaced Heywood and the side rallied, pulling a goal back and narrowly failing to save a precious point. It was not much, but it was something to build on. A fortnight later the long-awaited victory arrived – 22 games and the best part of eight months since the last one in League Two. Defying the bookies odds of 9-2 against a win, Grimsby shocked Bury at Gigg Lane with two goals in a five-minute spell in the first half. Liam Trotter and Nathan Jarman pounced to net the vital goals from close range and Grimsby ended the first half in buoyant mood, albeit with only ten men on the field, Kalala having received two yellow cards. The second period was all about hanging on for dear life, an achievement aided by the subdued home side, who were on a poor run of form at Gigg Lane. This was their fourth successive home loss, despite having topped the table earlier in the season.

Former Wolves and Sheffield Wednesday striker Adam Proudlock galvanised things in attack following his arrival on loan from Darlington and he was followed into the club by a man who had experience of leading the England attack – albeit only the once and more than twenty years earlier. Brian Stein was given the job of first-team coach and chief scout by the manager, who then attempted to land an even bigger fish when going after former Liverpool ace Robbie Fowler, offering him a player-coach role. For a spell the deal looked as if it would go ahead, only for Fowler, by now 33, to eventually decide to head for Australia after his contract expired at Blackburn Rovers. The prospect of a winter in Cleethorpes clearly held less appeal than a spell in tropical Townsville, where Fowler would turn out for North Queensland Fury in the A-League.

Now that the long run without a win was over, Grimsby experienced mixed fortunes, even tasting the luxury of three wins in a five-week period around the turn of the year. It was just enough to keep them out of the bottom two relegation places for now, but not enough to climb the table. An encouraging 3-0 triumph over Rotherham failed to kick-start the surge upwards that the fans desperately wanted to see, and February proved a particularly traumatic month, five successive defeats featuring in a run of nine games without a win.

After a home loss to divisional leaders Brentford at the beginning of March, Town found themselves overtaken by Bournemouth and sitting in 23rd place. There were a dozen games left and demotion out of the League was staring Grimsby in the face. Luton had earned themselves 40 points by now, but due to their 30-point penalty, remained in bottom place. Troubled Chester, meanwhile, were by now on a miserable run without a win (that would extend to nineteen games, eighteen in the league) and were slipping downwards in dangerous fashion. Luton looked unlikely to reach safety, so Grimsby's survival task looked fairly simple – merely concentrate on catching Chester, currently four points better off, but having played a game more.

The chances of escaping the drop received a thoroughly unexpected boost four days after the Brentford defeat, when mid-table neighbours Lincoln came to Blundell Park and were crushed by an astonishing late burst of four goals in the final twelve minutes. It was a surreal scene, reminiscent of the unexpected 6-0 thrashing of Boston which had also come out of the blue two years earlier, and which had coincidentally also been Grimsby's response to a losing run taking them down to 23rd place. Back in 2007 they'd followed the goal-fest by climbing well clear of danger. Could it happen again?

As a bonus, in terms of local bragging rights, the lashing of Lincoln just about killed off the Imps' lingering play-off hopes too. Hero of the hour was Adam Proudlock, who was recalled to the side to replace new signing Adrian Forbes. Proudlock grabbed a hat-trick and his strike partner Jean-Louis Akpa Akpro notched the other two, his first goals for the club. It was a remarkable contest, still deadlocked at 1-1 as the 80th minute approached. Twenty-four-year old Frenchman Akpa Akpro, formerly with Toulouse and FCM Brussels, and still finding his feet in

League Two, gleefully netted his first goal in English football and the whole game changed. Lincoln replaced a defender with a striker to try and save a point in the final minutes, but it was a gamble that backfired. The home side went goal-crazy, Proudlock twice converting passes from Danny Boshell, before Akpa Akpro bagged the fifth after a solo run. The smiles were as wide as the scoreline, a sight all too rare in recent times at Blundell Park.

Slipping up 1-2 in midweek at mid-table Chesterfield four days later didn't seem like the end of the world, for Grimsby now had to play the two sides they hoped were destined to fill the two demotion places below them – hapless Chester and desperate Luton. A minimum of a point against each would surely be the platform to eke out survival for another year?

Things didn't go quite according to plan. At Chester, Nick Hegarty took advantage of the capricious wind to collect the ball and drive it past the floundering home keeper. The lead was held for more than half-an-hour before Chester levelled through Ryan Lowe's neat finish to save a point. They had earlier gone agonisingly close when Town's new keeper Wayne Henderson appeared to carry the ball over his goal-line and then when Kevin Roberts blazed an easy chance over the Grimsby bar. Three days later the squad travelled south to play their game in hand on Chester, needing at least a point at Luton to enable them to climb out of the bottom two. Luton were at the bottom, fourteen points adrift, and knew that failure to beat Grimsby on this night would surely condemn them to the Conference.

It was Mike Newell's first return to his former club since they'd sacked him two years earlier. Back then many Luton fans had sympathised with Newell, who had been echoing their own concerns about where all the millions from player sales had gone at Kenilworth Road. But since those days they had begun to turn against him, angry he was suing their club for a six-figure sum, and over the revelations that his contract had stipulated he would personally profit from all those controversial sales that had denuded their successful side. In recent times the catastrophies at Kenilworth Road had been so manifold and complex that bitter home fans were quick to blaming just about everyone they could for their club's demise – and Newell was certainly no longer the noble moral crusader previously portrayed.

It promised to be a hot reception for the Grimsby boss, in a raucous atmosphere. Thick-skinned Newell said he wasn't at all worried and wouldn't be hiding. 'It's just another game to me,' was his throwaway line, presumably said with tongue firmly in cheek.

It was certainly a tasty confrontation at this crucial stage of the season and enlivened the taste buds of the national media. *The Times* was among those who made a rare foray down to the nether regions of the Football League to publish a lengthy match preview.

Grimsby recalled former Luton winger Adrian Forbes to their side, but this didn't take the heat off Newell, for Forbes was warmly applauded by Luton fans, who remembered his wholehearted displays, and all their ire was saved up for Newell himself. At one point he seemed to respond to the boos by holding up three fingers, perhaps indicating the three good seasons he had at Luton, but in the heat of the battle he wasn't about to receive any sympathy.

Ryan Bennett got free of his marker to send a looping header into the Luton net shortly before the interval, only for the nervous Hatters to produce an instant equaliser, Mark Bower's effort judged to have crossed the line before being booted clear. Amid much tension the second half remained deadlocked until the dying seconds. With Luton substitute Sam Parkin unsettling the visitors' defence, Asa Hall exploited the disarray to pounce and volley a last-minute winner that sparked scenes of jubilation. Luton were still a long way adrift at the bottom, but this result gave them an outside chance of catching Chester and Grimsby.

There were by now eight games to go, and Grimsby's task was to win three or four of these to ensure survival. They had not achieved such a winning ratio for a long time, however, so tension remained in the air. What Newell could probably have done without was the need to bounce back from the Luton defeat against a side from the top four – but that was Grimsby's fate the following week when Gillingham were in town. See 'Match of the Season' below.

Fans disillusioned by recent events would not have had their mood improved by the apparent poor communications at the club that week. An announcement appeared on the official website that players Phil Barnes, Tom Newey and Gary Montgomery's contracts had been cancelled by mutual consent – only for this to be hastily amended the next day to say that the trio were actually leaving because their services were no longer required.

The lack of clarity, not helped by Newell's comments on the issue, led to unconfirmed gossip that the trio had been booted out shortly before the Luton game for allegedly being disruptive and having an attitude problem. Onlookers wondering what exactly was going on behind the scenes might have been placated somewhat by the arrival of two good-looking signings at this point – the Leeds midfielder Peter Sweeney, and well-travelled Bradford City striker Barry Conlon.

The £5 admission offer at home to Gillingham was declared a big success and remained in place for the following game, against Aldershot
Town, and this helped bring in the biggest crowd of the season, topping
the 7,000 mark. The tension and high winds ensured it would not be a
classic, but the big crowd had no complaints by the end. More than 80
minutes of stalemate had been broken by new man Conlon driving a
penalty straight down the middle of the goal to give the club its first
back-to-back wins in two months. Yes, Grimsby were inching their way
to safety and the feeling of relief was palpable as fans streamed away
from the ground afterwards. Even local MP Austin Mitchell was able to
get home without taking the usual verbal stick from fellow fans about
how his presence at games brings them bad luck. The Member for Great
Grimsby had sponsored the match-ball for this game, and quipped afterwards: 'My staff tell me I've got to pay for it personally because, unlike
dirty videos, it's not a permissible MP's expense.'

So, by the end of March, with half a dozen games left, Grimsby's
prospects were much brighter, for although they remained in 22nd place,
just one above the drop zone, they were now three points ahead of
Chester and eleven of Luton. Significantly, sorry Chester hadn't won a
single league game since December and looked highly unlikely to mount
a late revival.

Helped in no small part by the morale-boosting presence of the lively Conlon, the Mariners went on to secure successive mid-April victories
over Notts County and Port Vale to make themselves all but safe, heading into the final fortnight of another traumatic season. Bournemouth
confirmed their own safety by beating Grimsby 2-1 in front of more than
9,000 in the campaign's penultimate game, but the welcome news filtered
through that Chester had only drawn with Aldershot that day. It meant
that only freakish results on the final Saturday would allow Chester to
beat the drop by overhauling Grimsby. They were three points behind the
Mariners and with a vastly inferior goal-difference – and both sides had
just one game each to go. Chester would need to overturn a nineteen-goal
deficit on the final day to pull the rug from under Grimsby. Luton by now
had succumbed to the inevitable and had fallen through the trap door in
24th spot.

The Blundell Park faithful were desperate to see the season out with
a win and urged the Mariners forward, but the final game with feeble
Macclesfield, who were only six points better off, turned into a forgettable affair, the point taken from a goalless draw ultimately proving academic, because Chester lost their game with Darlington and thus departed with a whimper. Newell had achieved his minimum aim, of steering

the club clear of relegation, but the overall mood was hardly one of jubi-lation. After all, 90th in the Football league represented Grimsby Town's worst finish position of all time. The only thing to celebrate was that Mike Phillips' sterling work on the Blundell Park playing surface had again won him the League Two Groundsman of the Year award.

The future looked uncertain as players and fans began casting their eyes towards summer holiday plans. The final team line-up of 2008-09 had been full of loanees and players who looked to have appeared for the last time for the club. A close season clear-out was indicated. Assistant manager Stuart Watkiss was not offered a new contract and would be replaced by Brian Stein, already on the books. The chairman explained that it was unsustainable for the club to effectively have two assistant managers and that Stein was Newell's preferred option.

Match of the Season 2008-09

GRIMSBY 3 GILLINGHAM 0   League Two, 21 March 2009

New signings Peter Sweeney in midfield and Barry Conlon in attack, plus excellent backing by a vociferous Blundell Park crowd, breathed new life into Grimsby and the challenge of promotion-chasing Gillingham was simply brushed aside. It was a day when the form book went out of the window and Town fans could at last smile again.

Gillingham arrived at Blundell Park in second place, with eight unbeaten games behind them. They had overturned the Mariners 3-0 at Priestfield early in the season, but – despite their elevated position – had a tendency to capsize occasionally on their travels. Gillingham had gone down 0-7 at Shrewsbury and 0-4 at Bury this season, and perhaps that gave grounds for faint optimism.

The terrific atmosphere generated by the biggest gate of the season thus far, who had taken advantage of specially reduced admission prices, spurred Grimsby forward and they twice stuck the woodwork in addition to knocking three goals in. The positive mood generated was liberating for the under-pressure players, and excessively so for one particular fan, who stripped down to just a T-shirt and 'streaked' across the pitch in bizarre fashion.

The Mariners deservedly went ahead just after the half-hour, when Jean-Louis Akpa Akpro reacted quickest after Nick Hegarty's shot had struck a post. Then Gills goalkeeper Simon Royce produced a fine save from a free-kick taken by Sweeney, the Glaswegian loanee from Leeds also hitting a post later in the game. Lively fellow debutant Conlon could have increased Grimsby's lead on more than one occasion, and was denied a clear penalty after being pushed to the ground in one incident.

A clever run by the tricky Agpa Akpro set up Hegarty on 57 minutes to roll home the crucial second goal, and the icing on the cake was duly added in stoppage time when Hegarty set up Conlon for a simple goal. It was sweet revenge for the earlier 0-3 defeat at Priestfield, and convinced any remaining doubters that Newell and his team were now in the right mood to end a bad season with a flourish.

The crowd's part in the win was highlighted by a number of sources. Gills boss Mark Stimson told reporters: 'They had a fantastic crowd here today and if their manager had that support every week I'm sure they wouldn't be where they are at the moment.'

Chapter 9

Chronicle of a Death Foretold

Coca-Cola Football League	2009-10
League Two (level 4)	23rd (demoted)
FA Cup	1st Round
League Cup	1st Round
Football League Trophy	3rd Round

JULY 2009

In deepest Devon, the omens for Grimsby Town's new season were beginning to look inauspicious. The touring Mariners squad found itself already encountering problems, even though the new season was still three weeks away. One would think gentle pre-season workouts near the picturesque harbours and clotted cream cafes of south-western England would be trouble-free affairs. But it was not so: the club was a participant in the curiously named Errea South-West Challenge Trophy, a tournament staged over several days in footballing backwaters such as Appledore and Great Torrington – seemingly an ideal low-key warm-up for the season proper. A chance to get the team away for a spot of team-bonding in pleasant surroundings. Or, at least, that was the general idea.

All was going well until the latter stages of this week-long tournament – even given the horrendous weather, which led to certain pitches becoming waterlogged. The trouble really began when Grimsby reached the final, only to find their opponents would be none other than Mike Newell's former club Luton Town. The Hatters were accompanied on this tour of the south-west by around 250 fans, who, to put it mildly, had already begun making life uncomfortable for their old boss. The upshot was that a dispute over kick-off times, plus concerns over the personal safety of Newell, led to Grimsby forfeiting their place in the final and walking out.

Perhaps when entering the competition Grimsby hadn't really expected to make the final and thus have to cope with four games in five days – the last of which would be just 24 hours before a Lincolnshire Cup contest with Scunthorpe more than 300 miles away. Told to take the field at 6pm on the Sunday evening to face Luton, there were anxious faces in the Grimsby camp, and an attempt was made to bring the kick-off forward, so they could at least get home in reasonable time to meet Scunthorpe. This request was refused, and Mariners officials promptly went into a huddle to discuss their next move. There was already anxiety that Luton's raucous band of fans might overstep the mark in their campaign of barracking Newell, for managers occupied a touchline area largely unprotected in these Spartan footballing surroundings. With two strong reasons not to play the final, it was decided that enough was enough and they would withdraw. So the Grimsby party high-tailed it to the nearest trunk road, leaving Luton without opponents to play. Belgian side Montegnee were hastily invited to fill the breach, despite the fact they had finished bottom of Group B, below Grimsby and Yeovil. A rather unsatisfactory sequence of events, but at least Grimsby left the tournament undefeated, three wins to savour, against the Belgians by 1-0, 3-2 over Yeovil, and 4-1 over Rushden & Diamonds in the semi-final. Rather predictably perhaps, the cup game that they rushed home to play ended in a 3-0 win for Scunthorpe.

AUGUST 2009

Any lingering bad feeling emanating from the Devon debacle was forgotten on the first day of this month, when a hastily arranged friendly at the little West Road home of Winterton Rangers finished in a landslide 12-1 victory. It was a highly positive, if freakish, way to wrap up another pre-season programme. A mismatch it may have been against opposition from the humble Northern Counties East League Premier division, but you can only beat what's put in front of you, and Town certainly enjoyed some good shooting practice. Seven of the goals came from the strike duo with vastly contrasting playing styles and hairstyles, Barry Conlon and Jean-Louis Akpa Akpro. Every silver lining surrounds a cloud, however, and Nathan Jarman would depart painfully from this walkover in the rain, suffering a suspected broken toe in the first half.

With the friendlies out of the way, most of the talk prior to the big kick-off surrounded a player who was staying put, rather than those who were going in and out of Blundell Park during the summer recess. The much-coveted defender Ryan Bennett was the subject of two big offers from ambitious Championship newcomers Peterborough, but talks broke down and Grimsby were able to tie their young but level-headed skipper to an improved four-year contract. It was a blow to Barry Fry and Darren Ferguson at Posh, but Town chairman John Fenty was understandably cock-a-hoop at keeping this young jewel. His mood was further enhanced by positive news about season-ticket sales, which showed a healthy increase, despite the gloom of recent times.

Fenty also revealed that the club had become stricter about ensuring its players lived locally, a policy that had proved to be a costly part of recent contract negotiations, he admitted. These talks had featured the likes of Irish goalkeeper Nick Colgan, a man of fourteen clubs, latterly Sunderland, who was recruited to go between the sticks. Newell was also allowed funding to sign up former loanees Peter Sweeney, Barry Conlon, Joe Widdowson and Adrian Forbes on a more permanent basis, and he bolstered the ranks further with ex-Luton and Barnet midfielder Michael Leary, defender Paul Linwood from Chester, and striker Chris Jones from Swansea.

The season proper began promisingly as Town took a first-half lead at Cheltenham, but a mystifyingly poor showing in the second period saw them overhauled 1-2. That result would come back to haunt Grimsby, for Cheltenham would survive, one place above the Mariners. Had Grimsby hung on to that half-time lead, Cheltenham would have been demoted at the season's end. A whole season encapsulated into 90 minutes.

A few days later a ten-minute spell of defensive mayhem allowed Tranmere to kick the Mariners unceremoniously out of the Carling Cup to the tune of 0-4. The manager and chairman both called for impatient fans to look on the positive side after this unfortunate start, but finding positives became a very tough task when freshly relegated Crewe then came to Blundell Park and hammered another four goals into the Town net. The visitors from Cheshire had twice as many goal attempts as Town, who had thrown on all three subs by the 49th minute in a vain attempt to turn the tide. It was not a pretty sight. Newell confessed this display was as bad as anything he'd been involved with, in more than five years as a manager – and he refused to make any excuses. It was certainly a league debut to forget for young goalkeeper Tommy Forecast, a 6ft 7in Londoner, rushed in on loan from Southampton to replace injured new-boy Colgan.

Football fans are known for their dark humour in adversity, and the deepening gloom at Blundell Park prompted one long-suffering individual to log on to the internet and launch a campaign to close down the club altogether! He wrote: 'The only way to end the misery that so profoundly blights our lives for three quarters of every precious year of our time on God's sweet Earth – is to close down Grimsby Town. Not convinced? Just imagine an existence free from all this pain. Imagine yourself liberated forever from this endless round of suffering and shattered hope . . . join the campaign to close down Grimsby Town FC right now and claim back your life from the grip of unending despair.'

Another defeat, 1-2 at home to Rotherham, followed, the four straight losses meaning Town had managed to start the season in even worse fashion than usual. The club's reputation for giving everybody else a head start in August was by now well deserved. Thankfully, relief was at hand – for the second season in succession – at the home of Bury, who had chalked up two wins out of three. Grimsby pinched the three points, Conlon's head powering home a first-half goal, this followed by some resolute defending to keep Alan Knill's men at bay. It was certainly not a game for the purists, but then nobody ever expected it would be.

The chairman spoke of his relief and praised the indefatigable supporters who made the trip to Gigg Lane, while Newell said it now felt as if the season had really started. But, typically, he was not getting carried away and confessed he and his new assistant Brian Stein were concerned over not getting the quality they expected at the moment.

Unfortunately Town weren't able to quickly build on their fleeting success on the road, and Aldershot came along to inflict a third successive home defeat, 1-2, on an afternoon which ended in a flurry of anger and red cards. The frustrated Conlon and sub Adam Proudlock were both dismissed after an unseemly melee, which at least gave them the opportunity to hide in the showers and avoid the cascade of boos at the final whistle. A month that had begun with twelve goals scored in one match thus ended in a state of deep depression. The bookies and pundits who had tipped Town for relegation had no cause to revise their opinions. Some onlookers even wondered whether certain members of Grimsby's squad were actually in the wrong sport – for the day after the Aldershot defeat, the team took part in a charity cricket match and full-back Robbie Stockdale shone with a brisk 49 runs and took 'a wonder catch', while young Grant Normington rattled up 30 runs on the first occasion he'd ever lifted a bat.

SEPTEMBER 2009

Giant goalkeeper Tommy Forecast, talked up as an England prospect when he first arrived, was sent back to parent club Southampton at this juncture, and Newell looked elsewhere for a custodian, finally settling on the Scunthorpe stand-in Josh Lillis, seven inches shorter than Forecast, but a tad more experienced. Newell shuffled his pack for the trip to Port Vale – apparently abandoning his much-favoured 4-4-2 formation – with Lillis debuting and skipper Matt Heywood making his first appearance of the season. The changes failed in a big way to stop the rot and Grimsby went under 0-4. It was another game capped by a sending off, and another in which the loyal travelling supporters struggled to find any encouraging aspects to cling to. One sounded desperate as he wrote afterwards: 'Tactical analysis is redundant, Town need a psychologist. What is in their heads, what is in their hearts?'

The Vale Park defeat had not merely been a bad day at the office, the problems apparently went far deeper. Straight-talking Mike Newell, to his credit, was in no mood to hide, and delivered an impassioned 'state of the nation' speech to the media: 'I've never experienced a period like this – it's been much the same since I took over last October. Too many people in and around the club accept defeat too easily – it's like a losing mentality. Look at the way we've started and yet there's been very little backlash from fans. I expect to get flak and for people to call for my head but that's hardly happened. I read a letter in the paper about the record over the last ten years and how the club has only finished above 15th place once in the last ten seasons. That is completely unacceptable, but it's as if that has led to people accepting a poor run – it's like they feel, because of the last few seasons, the start this season was to be expected. Well I'm not about to accept it – it's something that's been annoying me for some time and I'm determined to change this attitude around the place. I don't want anyone to accept us losing games and being in the position we are – either inside or outside of the club. I don't accept it, so why should anyone else. I'm not here to be Mr Nice Guy, I'm here to do a job and I'm determined to change this attitude. I'm fed up with shaking hands with opposition managers and saying 'well done' every week. Everyone needs to aim higher if the club is to get out of this rut. If that increases pressure on me to get results then that's fine – that's what my job is all about. People should have higher demands – this recent record in the last decade needs to end.'

Whether it was Newell's bold words, or perhaps the rumoured 'sacking' of a coach driver who was allegedly bringing the team bad luck, but results suddenly took a turn for the better in mid-September. In a contest devoid of any genuine excitement, Grimsby ground out a 1-0 home win over winless Hereford, thanks to a desperately late goal forced home by Danny North. The relief was palpable throughout the stadium and it was a case of 'never mind the quality, feel the three points'. Spirits were lifted and the impetus carried over to the long trip to Torquay a week later when another hard-earned clean sheet and two second-half goals flattened Paul Buckle's anxiety ridden Gulls, whose own losing run now stretched to five games. Luck that had previously deserted Grimsby was in evidence for the first goal at Plainmoor, the ball ballooning into the net off a defender. Grimbarians had a spring in their step once again, but Newell cautioned against getting carried away, saying the team was still not firing on all cylinders and that neither of the victories had been convincing. Nevertheless, nine points from eight games saw Grimsby three points clear of the drop zone with a visit from basement-club Darlington looming. It was never going to get any better than that all season.

Caution or not, even feisty Mr Newell couldn't resist a titter or two when news filtered through that England international Sol Campbell had quit fellow League Two side Notts County after just one game – largely because he couldn't tolerate the 'inferior facilities' at Meadow Lane. Newell reckoned Campbell would have left Grimsby even quicker, for things had got so bad at Town's training ground that the fire service were asked to come in and hose down the dangerous rock-hard surface. Meanwhile, as injuries to key players kept coming, it was tempting to wonder whether the training pitch might be to blame?

It was far too early to call it a six-pointer, but Grimsby's visit from Darlington was certainly a battle of strugglers. Darlington arrived with just one point and three goals from their eight league games and had yet to keep a clean sheet. Surely they were there for the taking. Youngster Bradley Wood was thrown into the fray for his Grimsby debut and won praise from all quarters in a disappointing 1-1 draw. Town had certainly been under pressure to beat the bottom-placed side, and were a goal up going into the last ten minutes, but the visitors were seemingly in an even tougher place – for within an hour of the final whistle, Quakers chairman Raj Singh decided that failure to win warranted sacking his manager Colin Todd. Having come from behind to equalise late on, while finishing the match with just ten men, Todd might have expected something a little more encouraging than his P45, but such is football.

Former England defender Todd thus became the ninth opposition manager in recent years to part company with his club following a failure to beat Grimsby. His predecessors were Graeme Sharp (Oldham), Steve Bruce (Huddersfield), John Ward (Bristol City), Gordon Strachan (Coventry), George Burley (Ipswich), Trevor Francis (Crystal Palace), Jimmy Quinn (Shrewsbury) and Terry Butcher (Brentford). It was becoming clear that club chairmen tend to reach a tipping point when their side cannot overcome the Mariners.

A midweek trip to Chesterfield saw a return to losing ways, Town clawing two goals back in the final twenty minutes, but still succumbing 2-3 to Lee Richardson's mid-table side. Ineffective formation and tactics, an apparent lack of motivation and poor refereeing were all put forward by frustrated fans as the key reasons behind another £16 admission fee being wasted.

OCTOBER 2009

Three days later the season reached a new low as Barnet eased their way to a 3-0 win over Town at Underhill, the afternoon being rounded off by a red card in the dying minutes for Town substitute Barry Conlon, his second of the season. More than 500 travelling Grimsby fans looked on in dismay. Barnet had, in fact, started the season like a train – this win lifted them to fourth – although their imminent collapse would see them almost demoted.

Then came a brief respite from league angst when a midweek trip to Hartlepool resulted in a 2-0 win before a thin crowd, but as this was 'only' a Johnstone Paints Trophy tie, even those whose glasses were half-full failed to get too excited. For Newell it was a pleasing outcome at the ground where his managerial career began in earnest.

But back where it really mattered, in League Two, Town found themselves in 22nd place and badly needing a win when league newcomers Burton Albion came to town, still with a spring in their step and enjoying the novelty of their new status. Burton bounced back well after Grimsby went ahead in the opening minutes when Polish goalkeeper Artur Krysiak blasted a back-pass against the back of Town striker Chris Jones and the ball span in to the empty net. Grimsby couldn't build on this stroke of good fortune and around the half-hour Paul Peschisolido's side had netted twice to take a lead they wouldn't relinquish. Serious-looking injuries to Adam Proudlock and Nathan Jarman only added to the local misery.

As the autumn chills began to bite, managers across the country were beginning to feel the draught, with a number already told to vacate their desks and hand back the company car keys – Bryan Gunn at Norwich and Peter Jackson at Lincoln among them. Newell, intriguingly, touched on the subject of his own future when penning his programme notes for the thirteenth league match of the season, a home encounter with Keith Hill's attractive Rochdale side. It wasn't entirely clear whether Newell was using the article to try and buy more time with his chairman, or with the fans – perhaps it was both? He wrote: 'When the results are poor the pressure builds on everyone, especially the chairman, and it results in panic buttons being pressed, as has happened elsewhere in the last few weeks. It is easy to stand alongside someone when everybody is buoyant and optimistic but not so easy when people are under fire. Supporters are ultimately the people with the most power, and also the people who are most entitled to their opinion, and they can influence anyone. Thankfully right now our chairman is stood alongside me, and not behind me. To be completely focused on what we are doing it has to be the case, otherwise you start looking at short-term solutions, which is not what this club needs.'

The chairman also appeared to be singing along to the 'stability' tune. He hinted that various under-performing players would be disposed of before any members of the management team. This, allied to the fact that the fans hadn't really turned against Newell in any concerted fashion, plus the realisation that sacking him might create a hefty compensation bill, gave grounds to believe Grimsby would buck the usual trend and stick with their manager through these troubled times. But such thoughts were soon found to be way off the mark. Just hours after Newell publicly lauded his chairman for standing alongside him, rather than lurking behind him, an almighty row apparently broke out between them in the Blundell Park boardroom. It was a flare-up that within 24 hours led to a parting of the ways.

The flashpoint had come immediately after Grimsby's fifth defeat in seven home matches so far, 0-2 to promotion-chasing Rochdale, a result that dropped them back into the bottom two. Town fielded three debutants (local lad Jammal Shahin and loanees Josh Magennis and Arnaud Mendy), but, frankly, they were simply outclassed. News that he had been sacked was telephoned to Newell the next day and was made public via the club's official website. A statement said Newell was departing due to 'irretrievable breakdown' – which, although a mite ambiguous, did confirm that bad results were not solely to blame. Newell would later challenge this decision legally, and would go into detail over what he alleged happened that evening in the fraught atmosphere of the boardroom.

But, for now, Fenty had to concentrate on steadying a ship in turbulent waters. He called upon youth team coach and former striker Neil Woods as caretaker manager, promoting him ahead of Newell's assistant Brian Stein. Woods had been a 'fantastic servant' to the Mariners over nearly twenty years and deserved this chance, pointed out Fenty. Meanwhile, Mike Newell rode off into the sunset, leaving a club on bad terms for a third time. At Hartlepool he'd only lasted six months, despite losing just seven of 29 games in charge, at Luton he'd won a healthy 83 out of 200 games, while at Grimsby he'd fared worst of all – winning only thirteen from 53 matches as manager.

If the players were demotivated by recent events, their mood won't have been helped when Newell was followed out of the club within three days by team captain Ryan Bennett, who was allowed to join Peterborough on loan, with a view to a big money permanent deal when the transfer window reopened in January. This came just eight weeks after Grimsby had firmly rebuffed two bids from Posh for the talented nineteen-year-old's services – obviously something had changed now that Newell was gone. Neil Woods thus found himself having to pick a side to tackle leaders Bournemouth at Dean Court without his skipper and a number of others due to suspension and injury. At least he could take heart from the positive attitude of the squad in training – extra sessions were happily undertaken apparently – and by the excellent away-fan support at Bournemouth. Life was proving difficult, but at least everybody appeared to be pulling in the same direction. Woods made a number of immediate team changes but, in the circumstances, the 1-3 defeat which followed was all rather predictable. It stretched Grimsby's losing league run to five.

The vacant manager's job allowed the local press and internet messageboards to have fun discussing candidates. One story which did the rounds was that the manager of the England women's team – Ms Hope Powell – was being considered. The 42-year-old Londoner was full-time boss of the women's national side, and had become the first female to gain a UEFA Pro Licence. It would indeed have been a delicious irony if Newell, who once proclaimed there was no place for women in senior football, were to be replaced by a female, but Town's chairman denied he'd ever met Ms Powell as suggested, and she hadn't applied, and the story died a death. Another name suggested by outsiders was that of Russell Slade, the former Grimsby boss (2004-06) who had recently been sacked by Brighton. Slade had done relatively well at Blundell Park, but was thought unlikely to return having been harshly treated by fans for much of his two-year stint.

Financially crippled Accrington Stanley provided Woods' first home opposition and under the Blundell Park Friday night floodlights Barry Conlon returned from the wilderness to save a point with a looping header just seventeen seconds from time. Grimsby ended this action-packed 2-2 draw with only ten men, but the fight shown by the team under the new manager was encouraging. The following day the two teams immediately above the Mariners – Torquay and Morecambe – both won, leaving Grimsby three points below the trap door. Morecambe's win was the first of seven in a row, which saw them leap up the table: they would finish the season fourth. Torquay would remain in danger all season, until sprinting to safety in their last eight games, all unbeaten.

Possibly the last thing Grimsby needed at this point was a tricky looking FA Cup clash with a team of minnows who were 38 places below them in the football pyramid.

NOVEMBER 2009

Blue Square Conference South side Bath City had made their way to the first round proper of the FA Cup by beating the humble trio of Willand Rovers, Bishop Cleeve and AFC Totton. A week before the meeting with Grimsby they'd failed to score at home to Bromley. Surely the Mariners had little to fear? Sadly, only the eager Jammal Shahin was able to raise his game for Grimsby, and the lively visitors cruised to a 2-0 victory thanks to Chris Holland's first-half header and a deflected shot by Darren Edwards after the break. To the embarrassment of the home contingent among a paltry crowd of 2,013, Bath's defence was rarely troubled all afternoon. Those Grimsby fans who stayed to the bitter end generously applauded the non-leaguers off the field, jeering their own men who slunk off red-faced. Apart from the inept display, the result was deeply distressing as it was guaranteed to make headlines nationally and get Grimsby the sort of coverage they could have done without on the TV highlights show that night. The club had suffered a succession of seasons featuring very low points, but these were surely new depths being plumbed?

Many fans were simply lost for words at how bad things had become. On the other hand, some were inspired to go public with their feelings. One anonymous supporter, known only by the nickname Poojah, published online a lengthy open letter of complaint, addressed to the team as a whole. Within days his astonishing rant received more than 100,000 hits on the fans site *The Fishy*, appeared on a further 100 UK football websites and was then picked up by sporting sites across the globe. Eventually it became a big hit on the social networking site *Facebook*, where it was described as 'arguably the best letter of complaint in history'. Before long it had attracted more than 12,000 *Facebook* 'friends', as people around the globe marvelled at the depth of raw feeling and angst that Grimsby Town and its decline had caused this writer. This was the letter:

'Dear Players of Grimsby Town FC,

'I am writing with regard to my absolute astonishment and disbelief as to the sheer magnitude of your complete lack of talent and failure to carry out the job for which you are paid to do. I am not aware of any swear word or other derogatory phrase in my current vocabulary which comes close to a description of your "performance" (and I use that term loosely) this afternoon [against Bath City], but let me just say that you have collectively reached a level of inadequacy and ineptitude that neither I nor modern science had previously considered possible.

'In fact I recall a time, in my youth, when I decided to call in sick at work and instead spent the entire day in my one-bedroom flat wearing nothing but my underpants, eating toast and ***** furiously over second-rate Scandinavian porn. Yet somehow, I still managed to contribute more to my employer in that one Andrex-filled day than your complete bunch of toss-baskets have contributed to this club in your entire time here.

'I would genuinely like to know how you pathetic little ******* sleep at night, knowing full well that you have taken my money and that of several thousand others and delivered precisely **** all in return. I run a business myself, and I believe I could take any 4,000 of my customers at random; burn down their houses, impregnate their wives and then dismember their children before systematically sending them back in the post, limb-by-limb, and still ensure a level of customer satisfaction which exceeds that which I have experienced at Blundell Park at any time so far this season.

'You are a total disgrace, not only to your profession, not only to the human race, but to nature itself. This may sound like an exaggeration, but believe me when I say that I have passed kidney stones which have brought me a greater level of pleasure and entertainment than watching each of you worthless excuses for professional footballers attempt to play a game you are clearly incapable of playing, week-in, week-out.

'I considered, for a second, that I was perhaps being a little too harsh. But then I recalled that I have blindly given you all the benefit of the doubt for too long now. Yes, for too long you have failed to earn the air you've been breathing by offering any kind of tangible quality either as footballers or as people in general. As such, I feel it's only fair that your supply runs out forthwith.

'I trust, at this precise moment in time, that [chairman] Mr Fenty is in his office tapping away on the easyJet web site booking you all one-way flights to Zurich, complete with an overnight stay with our cheese eating friends at Dignitas. Don't bother packing your toothbrush – you won't need it. In the event that our beloved chairman can't afford the expense (understandable given that he's soon going to have to assemble a new squad from scratch), then I am prepared to sell my family (including my unborn child) to a dubious consortium of Middle Eastern businessmen in order to pay for the flights. Christ, I'll drive you there myself, one by one, without sleep, if I have to.

'Failing that, understanding that most dubious Middle Eastern businessmen are tied up purchasing Premier League football clubs, I ask you to please take matters into your hands. Use your imagination, guys – strangle yourselves or cover yourself in tinfoil and take a fork to a near-by plug socket, or something. Just put yourselves and us fans out of our collective misery.

'So, in summary, you pack of repugnant, sputum-filled, invertebrate bastards; leave this club now and don't you ******* dare look back. You've consistently demonstrated less passion and desire than can commonly be found within the contents of a sloth's scrotum, so frankly you can just all **** off – don't pass go, don't collect your wages, don't ever come back to this town again. I look forward to you serving me at my local McDonald's drive-thru in the near future.

Yours sincerely,
A VERY DISILLUSIONED MARINER'

In comparison to the above, the reaction of the fans' website *Cod Almighty* was almost circumspect. Their spokesman reasoned that Mike Newell had at least been right about one thing – there was a negativity flooding through the entire club: 'There is a pandemic of misery throughout the club – you feel it in all contact with the club. It oozes from the walls. The club is limping along and no-one wants to give it a helping hand – why should they? It is a dying beast – bring in a vet or put it out of its misery.'

The run of games without a win was extended by a further three in the fortnight after the Bath City debacle. Town gave a decent account of themselves but went down to a straightforward 1-3 defeat at Leeds in the Johnstone Paints Trophy, and then forced two gritty goalless draws away from home at Northampton and Lincoln City. The latter saw debuts for loaned forwards Nicky Featherstone (Hull) and Michael Coulson (Barnsley), which, added to the five other new faces unveiled in recent weeks, meant Grimsby were fielding a much-changed outfit from the one taking the field barely a month earlier.

The two 0-0 draws hardly represented a rebirth, but there were enough positive signs to convince the men in the boardroom that Neil Woods should be given the manager's job on a permanent basis. The 43-year-old had a long and varied playing career, including eight years in Town's forward line, plus spells with Ipswich and Rangers, and was part of a footballing dynasty, his father Alan a former Spurs, Swansea and York City star, and his nephew Michael an England Under-19 international on Chelsea's books. The chairman called Woods 'a breath of fresh air' but his appointment after six games as caretaker without a win certainly surprised those who had expected a more experienced man to get the nod in these troubled times.

Chris Casper, a former Manchester United player whose career was ended by a broken leg at Reading, and who managed Bury for nearly three years, came in as assistant manager in place of Brian Stein. The appointments did not herald an immediate change of fortune and a dreadful display in a 0-3 pounding at home by Bradford City followed. A goalless draw at Macclesfield then restored a little pride, Town striking the woodwork twice.

DECEMBER 2009

During December Grimsby couldn't find a win for love nor money, but at least the new management team seemed to be making their struggling side a little harder to beat. As Christmas approached, Town shared the spoils with Dagenham & Redbridge, Shrewsbury and Morecambe, the latter on a bitterly cold Friday night. Sweeney's equaliser against Morecambe denied the visitors an eighth straight win. Despite making it four successive draws after that Bradford City hammering, Grimsby had only garnered seventeen points from 22 games. They were stuck firmly in 91st place in the league, only doomed Darlington beneath them, and looked one of the favourites to join them. The Mariners' main problem was clearly goalscoring, for only sixteen efforts had hit opposition nets by the end of that 22nd game. Cheltenham and Lincoln had replaced Torquay and Morecambe as the clubs within nearest reach. And this season, unlike the previous one, did not see Grimsby advantaged by huge point deductions imposed on three clubs. To that extent it was a level playing field.

As hefty bouts of pre-Christmas snow hit a shivering nation, Town's squad was forced to do what their footballing forefathers had often done, and hold training sessions on the nearby beach. Unfortunately the bracing winds lashing Cleethorpes didn't contribute towards ending the club's long winless run. Port Vale came to Blundell Park on Boxing Day bank holiday and beat a misfiring Mariners 2-1, after which Neil Woods held his hands up and confessed changes he'd made simply hadn't worked. Even Town's goal that day was merely academic – a penalty in the final minute of the final game of a horrible year (and of a horrible decade, all things considered). It was grim holiday fare for the faithful fans who by now hadn't experienced a home victory since 12 September. Even worse news came from down the A46, where fellow strugglers Lincoln had beaten Chesterfield 2-1 to pull five points clear of Town with a game in hand. The grim prospect of Conference football in the forthcoming new decade had taken a small step closer by the time Grimsby fans wearily raised their glasses that New Year's eve.

JANUARY 2010

Neil Woods' first transfer window as a manager witnessed a frenzy of activity. He began to clear the decks by allowing Danny Boshell, Danny North, Jamie Clarke, Barry Conlon, Grant Normington and Chris Jones to depart, and six new men were brought in to replace them, all making their debuts during January. But as Woods geared up his squad to renew the fight against demotion, he found he would be without winger Adrian

Forbes for many weeks. The former Norwich and Luton raider was livid about the situation for he had 'wasted five weeks' trying to recover from what was initially diagnosed as bruising, but which turned out to be a hairline fracture of his leg.

Getting busy in the transfer market means dealing with agents. Newell had hated doing this and, it seems, the men he left behind at Grimsby were struggling with it too. Statistics published nationally at this time detailed the amounts agents had been paid by the various clubs and Grimsby certainly wasn't the only place where these figures were greeted with astonishment. Chairman Fenty asked Grimsby fans to consider this, for example: the Mariners' total spending on the club's top ten transfers of all time (i.e. in 125 years) would only cover one-fifth of what Manchester City had spent on agents in one year! Premier League clubs had spent a total of £72 million on agents over a twelve-month period – money which had gone out of the game, but if spread among the hard-up Football League clubs would have given them all a life-saving £1 million each. It was a fair point.

Nobody expected Grimsby to splash the cash indiscriminately in these hard times, and the fresh signings that Woods was able to make looked promising in the circumstances. January saw the arrival of two 'permanent' captures and four more loanees, all of them brought in to pep up Grimsby's attacking options. Vastly experienced striker Lee Peacock, 33, had approaching 500 games to his name with the likes of Manchester City and Sheffield Wednesday and arrived from Swindon. This Rolling Stones fan, with a proven goalscoring record, was reportedly fit and raring to go following two operations on his spine the previous season. He was joined at Blundell Park by the former Leicester forward Tommy Wright, who had become disillusioned with life at Aberdeen, plus loanees Paris Cowan-Hall (Portsmouth), Wes Fletcher (Burnley), Ashley Chambers (Leicester), and midfielder Dean Sinclair (Charlton). In the last eight games of 2009 Grimsby had only managed three measly goals, so the new boys' task was crystal clear.

The new year started with a better display at home to Bury but the elusive first win in fifteen weeks failed to arrive, the Shakers saving a point with a last-minute penalty. This perked Bury up so much they won their next six games. Earlier in the match the unpredictable Jean-Louis Akpa Akpro had thanked Woods for recalling him by out-muscling a defender and lifting the ball over the keeper to put Town ahead. Grimsby then paid heavily for not adding to that goal in the chilly conditions.

The frost and snow created a break the following week. Over the winter, in fact, Grimsby got off fairly lightly with just two games called off

– Rotherham United, for example, were inactive for five fixtures in succession. Lowly Cheltenham came to Blundell Park in mid-January and escaped with a point, thanks largely to some fine saves by their goalkeeper Scott Brown. It was a game Grimsby dominated for long periods, and they had a one-man advantage after Ashley Eastham was sent off, but somehow the scoresheet remained blank throughout. Results elsewhere widened the gap from safety to six points. The Mariners were now in very serious trouble.

Woods shuffled his pack again and gave Chambers a debut at promotion-chasing Rotherham but the home side netted twice in the first half and were rarely troubled, the only consolation for 580 travelling fans being a neat injury-time goal from new-boy Fletcher.

A week later, Peacock, Wright and Sinclair were all introduced into the side for the trip to Aldershot Town, but a glorious chance to end the winless run was squandered when Proudlock blazed a penalty high over the bar five minutes from the end, following a handball offence. Town had forged an early lead when Michael Coulson's right-wing cross was deflected into the Shots' net, but had been pegged back by Kevin Dillon's men who applied plenty of pressure in the second half. It was a good point earned at the home of better-placed opposition, but Grimsby's need for three-point hauls was by now desperate. Somebody calculated that Town needed around 30 points from the last twenty games to survive – which was a tall order considering the haul before the Aldershot game was just nineteen from 26 matches, but at least the presence of a new-look forward line gave cause for some renewed hope.

FEBRUARY 2010

The visit of Sven-Göran Eriksson's Notts County pulled in an improved crowd as Grimsby entered the home straight in February. County boasted the meanest defence in the division. Town attacked their all-star visitors with vigour but sadly Wright and Peacock's lively home debuts didn't end in celebratory fashion. After a number of near-misses by the home side, County keeper Kasper Schmeichel launched a long clearance punt towards the Osmond Stand which reached the feet of League Two's leading scorer Lee Hughes. He sprinted for goal and finished expertly in front of the large band of jubilant away fans. Town were left pointless and the run without victory stretched to twenty league games.

The league position demanded that Grimsby must get wins soon, but at this crucial point in the season all their sweat and toil could garner was a series of well-earned draws – four in succession, in fact, including one in front of more than 11,000 at Bradford City, and another in the return game at promotion-chasing Notts County. At Meadow Lane, Lee Hughes nodded in his 23rd goal of the campaign early on, but debutant Jamie Devitt, a teenage Dubliner borrowed from Hull, curled in a fine equaliser on the stroke of half-time. Michael Leary produced a wonderful dipping shot from distance that crashed against the bar as Town strove in vain for a shock winner. Near the end, a dangerous challenge on Town keeper Nick Colgan saw Hughes red-carded and there were unsavoury scenes as he slowly left the field to the cheers of Grimsby's 700-plus travelling army. The improvement was there for all to see since the transfer window had closed, but unless a few wins came along soon, it was simply too little, too late.

The third of the quartet of draws would be the local derby at Blundell Park against Lincoln, one of the gaggle of lowly teams which might be seen as catchable in the closing weeks. Before the game, Chris Sutton's Imps stood ten points ahead of Town. Since Christmas they had chalked up four victories, which had helped lift them to nineteenth.

On derby day, local writer Pete Green reflected: 'We're way past optimism, but we hug pre-match pints in the knowledge that today's match and the visit of Macclesfield in midweek offer half a chance. Four points from these two games and we're still in it.' Barely three minutes were on the clock when Lincoln took the lead as Australian Chris Herd poked in from close range, but before half-time Lee Peacock got the final touch after a frenzied scramble and equalised. Grimsby's blood was up and, immediately after the break, attacking their favoured Pontoon end, Coulson burst forward to square for Peacock to net at the second attempt. It was a rare moment of delight for the home faithful and the first time Town had managed two goals in a game in nearly four months. A debatable penalty at the other end soon dampened spirits, however, with Colgan saving Brian Gilmour's first attempt, but unable to stop him netting the rebound.

Lincoln defender Adam Watts was carried off with a broken leg as things hotted up yet further, and the contest drew to a close with home fans in uproar over what seemed a blatant handball in the Imps area being ignored by the officials. As Lincoln's earlier penalty had been far from clear-cut, this decision seemed like a gross injustice and the under-fire referee received a frenzy of abuse. The blame for all Grimsby's ills of recent times, and beyond, were heaped on his shoulders as a red-hot local derby came to an end.

Once the dust had settled, the big question was whether the team could sustain the spirit shown against Lincoln when Macclesfield were the visitors three days later. The Cheshire side were another club mired near the bottom of the table, meaning this game perhaps qualified as a proverbial six-pointer. Added interest derived from the fact that the other two clubs Grimsby might catch (Torquay and Cheltenham) were meeting each other the same night. The prospect of a long-awaited win brightened near half-time when Devitt fired home a rasping effort, but this was cancelled out near the hour when Macclesfield's Richard Butcher curled a free-kick from 30 yards around the Grimsby wall and into the net, with keeper Colgan seemingly misjudging its flight. The division's two draw specialists duly ended the contest with a point apiece, meaning Town's winless run was extended to an horrific 24 games. Nathan Jarman's late sending-off only added to the air of gloom. Down in Gloucestershire that night, Cheltenham and Torquay also ended all-square at 1-1, meaning Grimsby remained five points below the safety line. It was still not an unbridgable gap by any means, but the majority of Town fans seemed to believe it was still far too wide for a team that was busting a gut, yet still only achieving draws at best.

Some tough games were on the horizon against teams in the top half of the table and, with March fast approaching, Neil Woods knew it would need an almighty effort, not to mention a change of luck, for Grimsby to set up any kind of close finish. At this point, perhaps the club could have done without the breaking news of Mike Newell's writ against them for wrongful dismissal. Various legal documents entered the public arena, reproduced in detail by the local media. Newell was suing for damages to the tune of £53,845.61, it was reported, and his evidence included allegations of a bust-up with the chairman and another director in the boardroom after the home defeat by Rochdale, disagreements over directors travelling on the team bus, plus Newell being prevented from signing Luton defender Lewis Emanuel. It was stated that Newell was suing for loss of earnings of £3,832.78 per month, and a further £25,000 he claimed he was due from the sale of Ryan Bennett to Peterborough, a transfer agreed by the club just hours after Newell was sacked.

(Note: In the summer of 2010, the whole matter would be settled out of court, Newell receiving a reported £5,000 in compensation – just a fraction of the sum he'd claimed. The club maintained it was in the wrong on only one issue – and that related to employment law.)

On paper, the team's trip to face Dagenham & Redbridge looked unlikely to yield much joy. Grimsby were unable to reproduce the passion of the last two home matches and the subsequent 0-2 defeat was all too predictable. 'Grimsby are all but gone in the relegation battle,' proclaimed the local *Telegraph* after this game. Following his blunder with the Macclesfield free-kick goal, Colgan had been dropped in favour of young

Mark Oxley, on loan from Hull. It had taken John Still's Daggers 49 minutes before they could beat him, Josh Scott diving to head home off the post with Oxley a helpless spectator. Grimbarians on this day-trip to the industrial end of Essex chanted optimistically 'We only want one win', but their hapless side failed to register a shot on target at a ground on which they had now failed to net in three visits. A fine solo run by winger Danny Green ended with a low shot across Oxley to make it 2-0 and end all hopes of a point. 'How much more can boss Woods take?' pondered the *Telegraph*. 'He's brought in new faces, discarded old ones, changed training and preparation, but none of it seems to be working. After a week of drama off the pitch, there was no saving grace on it and this particular soap opera is limping towards the worst possible finale.'

MARCH 2010

At long last! After a sequence of fifteen league draws and ten defeats in just under six months, Grimsby finally tasted victory again, surprising the bookies, and probably themselves, with a 3-0 thumping of promotion-chasers Shrewsbury Town at Blundell Park. It was Neil Woods' first win as a manager, and it renewed hope that an unlikely end-of-season revival might be on the cards. At this point, fellow-strugglers Cheltenham became the main focus of Grimsby's beady eye, as they were the only other club that looked like being realistically catchable. Sadly, Grimsby had already faced Cheltenham twice, picking up just one point. What they would have given for the chance to play those two fixtures again.

While Town were beating the Shrews, Cheltenham went down at home to Chesterfield, meaning just four points separated the two clubs, with both having played 34 games. Suddenly there was a little light at the end of the tunnel.

A foul on Akpa Akpro in first-half added time saw Dean Sinclair net a penalty against Shrewsbury, and for the first time in many months Town experienced the cushion of a two-goal lead when Sinclair tucked home the rebound after an Akpa Akpro effort was saved. Confidence returned in bucketloads, and the monkey was well and truly off the team's collective back when Akpa Akpro made it 3-0 with a a sweetly struck left-foot volley into the bottom corner after being played through by Peacock.

This long-awaited victory was followed by a 2-4 midweek setback at Crewe, and then a hard-earned point at Morecambe – Town's sixteenth draw of the season. The advent of three points for a win means that draws can be a curse. Had Grimsby won half and lost half of those sixteen draws they would have been eight points better off and outside the demotion places. If only!

The draw at Morecambe was spoiled by news that Cheltenham had achieved an incredible result at Burton Albion, scoring four times in the last six minutes to snatch victory from the jaws of defeat by the bizarre scoreline of 6-5. It extended their lead over Grimsby to six points and they now had a game in hand, as well as a superior goal-difference. The excitement generated in Grimsby by the win over Shrewsbury was by now evaporating.

In the build-up to the home game with Bournemouth, Woods had his back-up team bolstered by the addition of former Norwich and Wigan manager John Deehan, given the title of head of recruitment at Blundell Park. Deehan had been out of work for several months following the bizarre events at Kettering, where he had been ousted as assistant-manager for apparently making poor substitutions in an FA Cup defeat at Leeds and thus upsetting the Poppies' chairman. Some onlookers jumped to the conclusion that Deehan had been taken on at Grimsby as a ready replacement for the impending departure of Neil Woods, but the chairman firmly denied this – and indicated Deehan was signed mainly so they could make use of 'his bulging contacts database'.

Bournemouth lay second in the table, having conceded less than a goal a game all season. The lively atmosphere evident inside Blundell Park against Lincoln and Shrewsbury was again generated for the visit of the Cherries and it certainly helped inspire the players to rekindle the spirit needed for a great escape. Attacking the Pontoon end first, Jamie Devitt slammed Town ahead after Akpa Akpro's effort was parried by the visiting keeper, Iraqi-born Shwan Jalal. Town's tails were up and debutant Jude Stirling, on loan from MK Dons, nearly set up Rob Atkinson for a second, before the Cherries drew level through Lee Bradbury's header. A pulsating second half saw Town retake the lead when Coulson got the final touch with his chest after Peacock headed a Sweeney corner goalwards. The roar had barely subsided when Eddie Howe's men were again level, Liam Feeney's weak drive somehow squirming under the diving body of Colgan.

Coglan made amends with a fine save soon afterwards and Grimsby then found themselves with a one-man advantage after Cherries sub Jeff Goulding raised an elbow seconds after coming on and was promptly red-carded. With the seconds ticking away, Town grabbed their most dramatic winning goal in recent years, Coulson's 89th-minute cross zipping low across the box for substitute Ashley Chambers to hammer into the roof of the net.

The 3-2 win was just the tonic needed and with nine games to go Grimsby found themselves four points adrift of Cheltenham and safety.

A surge of renewed interest led to around 1,000 fans making the trip to Rochdale a week later. However, even pumped up from beating Bournemouth, the players couldn't rise to the occasion twice in eight days and the runaway league leaders cruised to a 4-1 win. It was a real anti-climax and even keeper Colgan admitted that all four goals conceded had been 'sloppy'. Chris Dagnall bagged a slick hat-trick for Keith Hill's side, and it wasn't difficult to see why there was now a 47-point gulf between these two teams. Nevertheless, Cheltenham lost at Macclesfield on the same day and Torquay went down at Morecambe, so all was still not lost.

APRIL 2010

Town needed to bounce back at home to resurgent Northampton (just two league defeats in nineteen games) on Good Friday and they certainly started brightly under the floodlights in front of a bumper crowd of 6,482, the highest of the season at Blundell Park thus far. But things began to go wrong when big Adebayo Akinfenwa set up Liam Davis to shoot the Cobblers ahead on eighteen minutes. A neat turn and shot by Coulson levelled matters before the break and Grimsby looked well capable of going on to win until defender Olly Lancashire was red-carded for alleged use of the elbow on Billy McKay. It was a debatable decision that even Cobblers' boss Ian Sampson thought was very harsh. Less than ten minutes after going down to ten men, Grimsby fell behind, Akinfenwa heading home a right-wing cross from Luke Guttridge. The desperate home crowd roared Grimsby forward in search of an equaliser, but there was to be no repeat of the late drama in the previous home game.

With their relegation rivals not playing till later in the Easter weekend, Grimsby now found themselves four points adrift from safety but having played two games more than Cheltenham, and six adrift of Torquay who had one game in hand. What was a bad situation promptly got much worse 24 hours later when both rivals won their home games against Lincoln and Shrewsbury respectively. Who would give a fig for the Mariners' chances now?

Defeat at mid-table Accrington Stanley on Easter Monday would surely put a cap on it. Some of the travelling die-hards knew they were probably only going to Lancashire to watch the beginning of the end of Grimsby's Football League life; the last few desperate twitches of a badly bruised corpse that had stumbled surprisingly to its feet in recent weeks, only to quickly slump back down again. Furthermore, judging by the collapse at Rochdale recently, there was unlikely to even be a noble death dance. But Neil Woods certainly had no intention of administering the embalming fluid just yet, and appealed Olly Lancashire's sending-off in the knowledge such an intervention would enable him to play at Accrington and thus improve Town's chances. The team carved out early opportunities at the sparsely attended Fraser Eagle stadium but failed to take any of them, and two goals conceded in a five-minute spell just before half-time had the travelling fans ready to administer the last rites on their club's League future. Billy Kee's header and Michael Symes' curling shot flashed past Mark Oxley to inflict what appeared at the time to be fatal damage.

But Grimsby can be relied upon, at least once a season, to spring the occasional shock and, after the interval, events proved there was life in the old dog yet. Stanley's purple-patch of five minutes was well and truly trumped when a rejuvenated Grimsby grabbed three goals between the 56th and 61st minutes. It created mayhem on the away terrace, turned the match entirely on its head, and breathed new life into the battle for survival. Coulson whipped in a good cross from the right for Mark Hudson to head his first goal for the Mariners since joining from Gainsborough Trinity a few weeks earlier. The impressive Coulson then won a free-kick which he took himself, rifling the ball into the net with the aid of a deflection. There was no stopping Grimsby now, and what would prove the match-winner was a truly superb goal, Devitt curling a left-foot shot into the net after an Akpa Akpro lay-off. Some desperate defending kept the lead intact, and once again Grimsby fans everywhere were sneaking a peek at the league tables with renewed hope in their hearts.

Neil Woods refused to set a points target for survival, insisting that all he was concentrating on was achieving one more point than Cheltenham or Torquay, who had won and drawn, respectively, that same day. The gap was now seven points, but Grimsby still had half-a-dozen games left, one of them at home to Torquay. Woods added: 'Over the last three or four months we haven't given many games away cheaply – the players have shown the supporters that they really care and believe they can get out of it. This [result at Accrington] will give tremendous heart to everybody. It will prove to supporters that we're not going to roll over and make it easy for people, and it proves to the players what they're capable of. The players and staff have always believed we can survive.'

And so, with Easter out of the way, it was time to pause and assess how things stood in the relegation battle. The win at Accrington had got the adrenalin flowing again, and Woods and his men looked up for the fight, even though the odds were still stacked against them. The run of 25 games without a win had been crippling, but not yet fatal. If past seasons were anything to go by, a final total of 50 points would surely guarantee survival, but as little as 46 or 47 might be enough. So four wins from their final six games could do the trick for Grimsby, and now that minds seemed properly focused, such a finish might just be possible. Of course, as well as maintaining the momentum of their second-half display at Accrington, Grimsby also needed their immediate rivals to stumble on their way down the finish line.

Long-in-the-tooth Grimsby fans were not surprised to find the season lingering on in this fashion. 'It's not the despair that kills you, it's the hope,' was the well-worn phrase that sprang to mind for many of them. One of them wrote: 'I fully believe this season will again go down to the final two games – and that's not to suggest we'll stay up, or even have a realistic chance of staying up – but that it won't be mathematically over until the very end. Just that little bit of hope – just a grain, to keep you hanging on . . . it would be typical Town to pull ourselves briefly out of this mire right near the end, before slumping back down.'

Woods and his squad needed to distance themselves from this mixture of anxiety, hope, and cynicism and get on with the business of chalking up more points. The first task after Easter was to achieve something that hadn't been done by a Grimsby team in nearly two-and-a-half years – victory in back-to-back away games. Around 300 Town fans set off southwestwards on the 400-mile round-trip to Hereford, glad to be facing a side floating around aimlessly in lower mid-table, although slightly concerned to find the Bulls had won four games in a row since Graham Turner had retaken the managerial reins at Edgar Street.

Experienced Nick Colgan was back in goal for Grimsby, despite apparently not being fully fit, and the attitude of the team couldn't be faulted as they produced a fine first-half display, leaving onlookers in no doubt which of the two teams still had something to play for. Jamie Devitt, scorer of the classy winner at Accrington, repeated the trick here in the early stages, curling home a fine shot, and Hereford rarely threatened to equalise. The only real moments of concern came late on when Hereford failed to convert after a lengthy goalmouth scramble, and when Colgan handled outside his box, but was shown a yellow card rather than red.

The delight among Grimbarians lasted until the final scores from elsewhere were confirmed. Incredibly, both Torquay and Cheltenham had not only won, they'd scored five goals apiece, the Gulls nap hand coming against league leaders Rochdale. So, after all that effort and improvement, poor Grimsby found themselves still seven points adrift of safety, and fast running out of games. Match-winner Devitt said: 'The lads were dejected because the other results just didn't go our way. The gaffer is trying to lift us all.'

Bottom six, after matches played on 10 April 2010

	P	Pts	GD
19 Lincoln	41	46	-19
20 Barnet	40	45	-9
21 Torquay	41	44	0
22 Cheltenham	40	44	-11
23 GRIMSBY	41	37	-24
24 Darlington	39	23	-46

Four wins from eight matches had followed the 25-game winless streak, meaning if Grimsby were on their way out, at least they were now making a reasonable fist of it. It had been a huge effort to overcome Accrington and Hereford on their own grounds, but could the team sustain this level of motivation three days later at home to Chesterfield, a club just outside the automatic promotion places, and therefore with their own fish to fry? Nearly 6,000 rolled up on a cool, clear Tuesday evening to find out.

For an hour everything went swimmingly. Town were by far the better side and attacked hungrily, deservedly taking a 2-0 lead, thanks to his first goal in eleven appearances for Tommy Wright, and another from Akpa Akpro. Grimsby found themselves with roughly half-an-hour to keep the Spireites at bay and the three points would be theirs. The great escape could still be on.

But anyone who thought Chesterfield would lay down and die at this point had forgotten about the dreaded curse of the former player. Step forward Jack Lester, a skilful forward, nurtured, developed and hero-worshipped in Grimsby for six years back in the days when the Mariners were not in such dire straits.

These days Lester was a mature 34-year-old wearing the No 14 shirt of Chesterfield – and he pounced twice in the final 25 minutes of this game to score the goals that rescued a point. Grimsby had put up a terrific fight, but failing to win from 2-0 up left the Blundell Park faithful in a state of anguish and despair. Michael Coulson was bundled over near the end, but loud penalty claims were brushed aside and Town had to be satisfied with a single point. They weren't relegated yet, but failing to take all three points here represented a very serious blow. Neil Woods wasn't the only one who had known all about the Lester factor: 'Jack's the best striker in this league for me. He's been a top quality striker for a long time. If anything drops in the box, from the opposition's point of view he's the last one you want the ball to drop too, because he is a calm head and a good finisher.'

So, whither Cheltenham, Barnet and Torquay on this evening, those other clubs attempting to flee the spectre of demotion? Cheltenham ground out a goalless draw at Shrewsbury, Barnet suffered a 1-4 thumping at Dagenham & Redbridge, while Torquay followed their hammering of Rochdale with another shock victory, 2-0 at promotion contenders Aldershot. The gap to safety was therefore still seven points. It was now looking as if Grimsby's only realistic chance of escaping the drop involved catching Barnet, for Ian Hendon's Underhill side were on a dreadful slide. Fourth in October, they had dropped into the bottom half in December, and were now 22nd, their lowest position all season. They also had the toughest-looking run-in and, importantly, would be meeting Grimsby in the penultimate game of this nerve-wracking campaign.

Bottom six, after matches played on 13 April 2010

	P	Pts	GD
19 Torquay	42	47	+2
20 Lincoln	42	46	-21
21 Cheltenham	41	45	-11
22 Barnet	41	45	-12
23 GRIMSBY	42	38	-24
24 Darlington	40	26	-45

Four Saturdays remaining, four games to go, and Grimsby probably needed to win all of them. It was the tallest of tall orders. Woods put a predictably brave face on the situation: 'We have to win four games and, yes, we believe we can do it. There is the spirit here to do it. We can do it, we need a bit of luck – needing teams around us to slip up – but we are capable of winning the four games in the form we are in. You've got to give Torquay credit, they've produced some terrific results. I'd rather be in their position than ours, but all we can do is keep trying to win games of football. It's taken out of our hands now, but we still have our job to do and we have to make sure we do it. There are another couple of clubs that aren't in form that will be looking over their shoulders now.'

Torquay came to Blundell Park for a match that just a few weeks ago was being described as potentially a 'winner takes all' scenario, but the Gulls' recent surge (ten points from four matches) had changed all that. Now they needed just a point to ensure Grimsby couldn't overhaul them, even if the Mariners then won their final three games. Paul Buckle's men were full of confidence, if such a thing were possible for a team nineteenth in League Two. Grimsby, on the other hand, had to take the pitch with the soul-destroying knowledge that even four wins out of four could be insufficient if others picked up points. To an unbiased outsider, the club's chances looked to be receding as fast as Gordon Brown's prospects in the forthcoming General Election. Many Town supporters already saw relegation as an inevitability and just wanted to be put out of their misery, but while survival was mathematically possible the calculations and the permutations continued to be discussed.

Pre-match noises were made about it being 'the most important game in Grimsby's history', but this was really just desperate hype designed to motivate players and supporters. Once things got underway, Torquay kept Grimsby at bay with some ease throughout the first half, and eight minutes after the interval came the match's turning point. Olly Lancashire tangled with Elliott Benyon in the box and the well-placed referee pointed to the spot. Nicky Wroe netted the kick straight down the middle and Grimsby shoulders slumped. Skipper Lee Peacock was immediately introduced as a sub but before long the lead had been doubled, Benyon hammering his fifteenth goal of the season.

Home fans began venting their fury on their chairman, and some were even seen departing early, even though the best part of half-an-hour remained. Torquay's big defender Guy Branston received his marching orders after a second caution, but it made little difference and their third goal was slotted in by the lively Gambian-born Mustapha Carayol after a long run. That was the final straw for many Grimbarians, who flooded towards the exit. The final whistle signalled a pitch invasion by around a hundred mainly younger fans who decided it was appropriate to head towards the celebrating Torquay fans and vent spleen at them.

Now it really seemed as if the fight was all over bar the shouting, and goalkeeper Colgan virtually admitted as much: 'We were meant to be fighting for our lives, our careers and families. I'm embarrassed. There should be pride in not wanting go out of the league.' Elsewhere, Lincoln lost at Shrewsbury and Barnet went down at Bradford City, so the game wasn't up entirely – but these helpful results did little to help Town fans' general mood.

Bottom six, after matches played on 17 April 2010

	P	Pts	GD
19 Torquay	43	50	+5
20 Cheltenham	42	46	-11
21 Lincoln	43	46	-22
22 Barnet	42	45	-13
23 GRIMSBY	43	38	-27
24 Darlington	41	26	-47

Grimsby, it seemed, were set to follow the likes of Luton, Wrexham, Mansfield and York out of the Football League, and the prospect of another old stalwart club dropping sadly into the Conference whetted the appetite of the national media. *The Mirror*, for example, took a close look at Grimsby's plight in the build-up to the trip to already relegated Darlington, the Town's 44th match of this traumatic season: 'To all but the most defiant fishmongers, it will be not so much an away trip as a voyage of the damned,' wrote columnist Mike Walters. 'After 121 years, Grimsby Town will slip out of the Football League if they fail to win at doomed Darlington, who have already slipped through the trapdoor. If the worst happens, it will be a good day for grown men to blub into their replica shirts – and there will certainly be plenty of room inside the Quakers' white elephant stadium for supporters on both sides to cry at each other.'

Chairman Fenty was portrayed as a lifelong fan who had built up a £20 million fish empire on the Humber quayside, who had not given up all hope of a miracle, but was bracing himself for doomsday: 'This club has a fantastic history, and the cast of famous names who have passed through Blundell Park – from Graham Taylor as a player to Lawrie McMenemy as a manager – only makes our plight harder to bear,' Fenty told *The Mirror*. 'As chairman, and as a fan, I could not be more disappointed and hurt to look at the League table and see the position we are in, and it has left me massively dejected . . . I don't blame our manager, Neil Woods, for the club's plight. He inherited a hugely difficult position, with question marks over the squad's fitness and the quality of certain players. He took over a weak side who were shipping goals and immediately turned them into a more resolute side who locked up the shop, but unfortunately we were not able to turn a dramatic improvement in performances, and a whole sequence of draws, into wins. Relegation, if it happens, would come down to a whole cocktail of things, but whatever happens we will look to the future and come back stronger.' Commenting on the way the recession had left his new stadium plan 'marooned in the pending tray', he said: 'We need to leave the nostalgia of Blundell Park behind us and move on. Sadly the retail market collapsed when the economy took a dive, but there is a real opportunity for the scheme to go ahead when it recovers.'

With the home side in 24th place and already doomed, surely the trip to Darlington was a game where Grimsby could salvage some pride and keep alive what were now wafer-thin hopes of survival? Around 500 fans travelled to the Quakers' huge and vastly under-populated arena looking for a third successive away win that would at least take the survival battle into May. The start they wanted was granted when Lancashire headed home a corner, and Akpa Akpro turned and swept home another flag-kick just before the interval. The party was in full swing among the travelling fans and noise levels went up a notch when news came through that Barnet were losing at home to Rotherham. A quick calculation revealed that if today's scores remained the same by the end, and Barnet lost their game in hand (away to Accrington), and then Grimsby beat the north Londoners at Blundell Park next Saturday – all of a sudden that huge gap to safety would be down to one single point going into the final day. Who said it was all over?

Both second halves did indeed remain goalless, meaning the gap was now down to four points. Barnet travelled nervously to Lancashire on the Tuesday night, to play their game in hand, knowing that victory would secure their safety and condemn the Mariners. A stalemate lasting 70 minutes ensued, before Accrington sub Billy Kee tapped in a cross from Michael Symes to net a winning goal that brought hope flooding back into Grimsby hearts many miles away. Now Barnet's trip four days later to Grimsby really did matter after all.

Bottom six, after matches played on 27 April 2010

	P	Pts	GD
19 Macclesfield	43	53	-7
20 Lincoln	44	49	-21
21 Cheltenham	44	47	-12
22 Barnet	44	45	-15
23 GRIMSBY	44	41	-25
24 Darlington	44	27	-54

MAY 2010

Barnet, and their chairman Tony Kleanthous, prepared for the big game at Grimsby in unexpected manner. They sacked their manager Ian Hendon. He was told shortly after arriving home during the early hours of Wednesday morning from the Accrington defeat. Poor results, in particular the current run of five successive defeats, were blamed, and it was announced their former boss 60-year-old Paul Fairclough was coming back to take charge of the club's final two games of the season. To add to the Bees' woes, they now faced a defensive crisis, with centre-backs Daniel Leach and Ismail Yakubu unable to play at Grimsby due to food poisoning and a bad back, respectively. Grimsby fans, who thought things were bad at Blundell park, were stunned by all this news. It seemed as if their opponents were imploding before a ball had been kicked.

Grimsby had been in 91st position in the League without a break since October, more than six months earlier. It had been a long, relentless ordeal, but now there was a pin-prick of light visible at the end of the tunnel and this helped create an upsurge of interest in this penultimate week of the campaign, leading to more than 7,000 turning up for the showdown with troubled Barnet. The tension was almost unprecedented, certainly in recent seasons, and it emerged that in the home dressing room Woods had dramatically 'made a pact' with his men that if the club was to be demoted, it simply must not be allowed to happen in front of the home fans here today. Nearly 500 Barnet supporters bravely sang their songs of defiance from the Osmond stand, but it was the Grimsby voices that carried more swagger and confidence despite their team's more perilous position.

Despite Town's Mark Hudson failing to score when clean through on goal, first blood in this battle to stay alive was not drawn until almost an hour had passed. Following a corner, Peter Bore swung a clearance back into the danger area and defender Mark Atkinson controlled the awkward ball on his chest like a seasoned striker, swivelled and smashed it past the Barnet keeper. His last goal had been eight months previously. It all happened at the Pontoon end and sparked frenzied celebrations that barely died down for the rest of the game. The goal had come just a couple of minutes after the same man tugged the shirt of veteran Paul Furlong at the other end, a clear penalty offence that, had it been spotted, might have changed everything. Such is the thin line between success and failure. Colgan had to make two crucial saves from Barnet's Mark Hughes before Hudson got clear again, in added time, and fired emphatically into the far corner. It clinched victory, took the fight until the final day, and prompted a major pitch invasion. Mounted police, plus a bout of booing from fans in the stands, eventually persuaded the invaders to withdraw so the game could be finished.

Barnet had pottered along all season playing before tiny crowds and subdued atmospheres, and today's occasion was just too much for them, coming as it did on top of their run of five straight defeats. 'It was like a gladiatorial ring,' reflected a shell-shocked Paul Fairclough. 'It was a full house and I think the Grimsby crowd made the difference today.'

Were Grimsby merely prolonging the agony for their long-suffering supporters, or did they really have a chance of producing the great escape on the season's very last day? They now possessed 44 points, one behind hapless Barnet, but had a goal-difference that was six inferior. It meant they had to win at Burton Albion and hope that Barnet would do no better than a draw at home to already promoted Rochdale, who had gone off the boil. If Grimsby were to draw, they could only survive if Barnet went down by seven clear goals. But if Barnet were to win, Grimsby were down whatever their own result at Burton. Of the two clubs, the Mariners could at least claim to be the form team, having won four and drawn one of their last six, the Bees losing all their previous half-dozen.

Bottom six, after matches played on 1 May 2010

	P	Pts	GD
19 Macclesfield	45	53	-9
20 Lincoln	45	49	-17
21 Cheltenham	45	47	-17
22 Barnet	45	45	-17
23 GRIMSBY	45	44	-23
24 Darlington	45	30	-52

Match of the Season 2009-10

BURTON ALBION 3 GRIMSBY 0   League Two, 8 May 2010

Around 2,100 Grimsby fans headed for the five-year-old Pirelli Stadium to be part of this last-day drama, an occasion that would decide whether 99 years of continuous Football League membership was at an end. Most thought they'd never see a day like this, following the mid-season winless run which, by the time it had reached 25 games, had indicated relegation would be done and dusted by Easter. Thanks to performances in recent games, if Grimsby were bowing out, at least they were not going with a whimper.

Burton were probably ideal opponents to face for this dramatic show-down. Their first season of Football League membership had gone well. They would finish mid-table, so had no higher aims against Grimsby than to perform well. They had lost more home games than they had won and were also a hit and miss side. Only four teams in League Two had scored more goals and only three teams conceded more. Burton's defence was even leakier than Grimsby's. Their season had also been peppered by crazy scores. They had won and lost games 5-2, and had chalked up 6-1 and 4-3 wins. Nor had they been content with four games yielding seven goals each. Eleven were scored in the home game against Cheltenham, and this is where Grimsby fans reckoned Burton owed them a favour. Cheltenham's four goals in the last six minutes had turned certain defeat into an eye-watering 6-5 win. Those three unexpected points were all that prevented Cheltenham from joining Grimsby on the 44-point mark.

However, such comforting thoughts were cold comfort once Burton punctured all the optimism by taking the lead with only ten minutes on the clock. Even worse, the goal came less than a minute after Jean-Louis Akpa Akpro had hit the post at the other end.

Greg Pearson curled the ball home from 25 yards and the hope that had recently built up began to slither through Grimsby fingers like fine sand. Burton manager Paul Peschisolido had called up goalkeeping coach Kevin Poole, now 46 years old, to go between the home sticks, and Poole seemed determined to play a starring role in this, possibly the last game of his 28-year career. Poole would end up making four first-class saves and riding his luck when other efforts struck his post or were cleared off the line. By the time Shaun Harrad grabbed a second Burton goal before half-time, most Grimsby fans had given up the ghost anyway. 'Whatever will be, will be, we're going to Salisbury . . .' came the darkly humorous chant from behind the East Stand goal.

Sadly a number of other visiting fans were not so tolerant of their club's fate. The atmosphere turned nasty and the prospect of a series of pitch invasions began to look highly likely. There were even fears some idiots might turn on their own players after the game, and when Harrad converted a 57th-minute free-kick to end all hope at 3-0, his celebration carried him among stray invaders near the main stand. Colleagues had to drag him away from what could have become an ugly incident, and the player later played down reports that he had been kicked by Grimsby pitch invaders. Scores invaded the pitch on the final whistle, jostling with police and damaging advertising hoardings. It was reported that at least twenty Grimsby fans were forcibly ejected from the ground and there were twelve arrests.

Burton boss Peschisolido sympathised: 'I feel for Grimsby – it's not nice seeing anyone relegated and I wouldn't wish that on anyone. To be fair they had a real go at us but [46-year-old] Kevin Poole was incredible. I don't know what he's eating, but to pull off stunning save after save like he did was brilliant. Some were world class.' Few seemed to notice, or even care, that down in Barnet the home side had scraped a 1-0 victory over Rochdale with a last-minute winner, meaning the Burton defeat was now an irrelevance anyway – Grimsby would have been doomed even had they won.

Chairman Fenty apologised for the 'few idiots' associated with the club, while skipper Peacock generously argued that it was only natural that the supporters felt angry, 'because relegation is soul-destroying and hurts both mentally and physically.' David McVay, a former Notts County player employed by the *Daily Telegraph*, reckoned Grimsby had retained a dignified presence in the Football League for a century, but thanks to these troublemakers had now relinquished that membership in disgrace.

For the hundreds of decent, law-abiding Grimsby fans in Burton's ground that afternoon, the sight of their fellow supporters besmirching the club's name was merely the latest depressing episode at the end of an awful decade. For the best part of ten years Grimsby Town had been in serious decline and for the last three seasons had lingered near the foot of League Two, flirting with the danger of dropping out of the League. Now such a fate had become an ugly reality.

Bottom six, after final matches played on 8 May 2010

	P	Pts	GD
19 Macclesfield	46	54	-9
20 Lincoln	46	50	-23
21 Barnet	46	48	-16
22 Cheltenham	46	48	-17
23 GRIMSBY	46	44	-26
24 Darlington	46	30	-54

Guide to Seasonal Summary

Col 1:   Match number (for league fixtures); Round (for cup-ties).
         e.g. 2:1 means 'Second round; first leg.'
         e.g. 4R means 'Fourth round replay.'

Col 2:   Date of the fixture and whether Home (H), Away (A), or Neutral (N).

Col 3:   Opposition.

Col 4:   Attendances. Home gates appear in roman; Away gates in italics.
         Figures in bold indicate the largest and smallest gates, at home and away.
         Average home and away attendances appear after the final league match.
         N.B. Home attendances are those registered with the Football League
         and should be taken as accurate.

Col 5:   Respective league positions of Grimsby and their opponents after the match.
         Grimsby's position appears on the top line in roman.
         Their opponents' position appears on the second line in italics.
         For cup-ties, the division and position of opponents is provided.
         e.g. 2:12 means the opposition are twelfth in Division 2.

Col 6:   The top line shows the result: W(in), D(raw), or L(ose).
         The second line shows Grimsby's cumulative points total.

Col 7:   The match score, Grimsby's given first.
         Scores in bold indicate Grimsby's biggest league win and heaviest defeat.

Col 8:   The half-time score, Grimsby's given first.

Col 9:   The top line shows Grimsby's scorers and times of goals in roman.
         The second line shows opponents' scorers and times of goals in italics.
         A 'p' after the time of a goal denotes a penalty; 'og' an own-goal.
         The third line gives the name of the match referee.

Team line-ups: Grimsby line-ups appear on the top line, irrespective of whether
         they are home or away. Opposition teams appear on the second line in italics.
         Players of either side who are sent off are marked !
         Grimsby players making their league debuts are displayed in bold.
         In the era of squad numbers, players' names are positioned as far as
         possible as if they were still wearing shirts 1 to 11.

Substitutes: Names of substitutes appear only if they actually took the field.
         A player substituted is marked *
         A second player substituted is marked ^
         A third player substituted is marked "
         These marks indicate the sequence of substitutions.

N.B.   For clarity, all information appearing in italics relates to opposing teams.

Manager: Mike Newell > Neil Woods

Results

No	Date	Att	Pos	Pt	F-A	H-T	Scorers, Times, and Referees
1	A CHELTENHAM 8/8	3,654	L	0	1-2	1-0	Conlon 35 / Ridley 56, Hayles 68 — Ref: D Sheldrake
2	H CREWE 15/8	5,007	24	0	0-4	0-2	— / Zola 34, 45, Jones 47p, Moore 90 — Ref: M Haywood
3	H ROTHERHAM 18/8	4,156	24	0	1-2	0-0	Sweeney 64 / Le Fondre 53p, Cummins 67 — Ref: G Salisbury
4	A BURY 22/8	2,799	20	W 3	1-0	1-0	Conlon 20 — Ref: R Booth
5	H ALDERSHOT 29/8	3,757	22	3	1-2	0-1	Conlon 81 / Donnelly 27, 49 — Ref: P Quinn
6	A PORT VALE 5/9	5,056	23	3	0-4	0-1	— / Dodds 43, Richards 68 [Heywood 87 (og), Collins 90] — Ref: G Eltringham
7	H HEREFORD 12/9	3,173	21	W 6	1-0	0-0	North 88 — Ref: J Waugh
8	A TORQUAY 19/9	2,575	18	W 9	2-0	0-0	Nicholson 47 (og), Sweeney 65 — Ref: O Langford
9	H DARLINGTON 26/9	4,014	17	D 10	1-1	1-0	Atkinson 21 / Main 81 — Ref: S Mathieson
10	A CHESTERFIELD 30/9	3,329	21	10	2-3	0-1	Proudlock 70, Sweeney 87 / Niven 30, Lester 54, McDermott 69 — Ref: D McDermid
11	A BARNET 3/10	2,497	22	10	0-3	0-2	O'Flynn 11p, Adomah 16, Bolasie 67 — Ref: D Sheldrake

Squad numbers in use (starting XI — Town above / opponents italic) and subs used

1 — CHELTENHAM (A)
Town: Colgan, Stockdale, Widdowson, Bennett, Atkinson, Sweeney, Jones*, Boshell, Proudlock, Conlon, Hegarty^
Cheltenham: *Brown, Bird, Ridley, Paak, Duff, Diallo, Hutton, Gallinagh, Richards, Hammond^, Bazanic**
subs used: Akpa Akpro^/Fuller · Hayles/Alsop

2 — CREWE (H)
Town: Forecast, Stockdale, Widdowson, Leary, Atkinson, Sweeney, Fuller*, Boshell, Conlon, Akpa Akpro*, Hegarty^
Crewe: *Button, Brayford, Jones^, Schumacher, Ada, Worley, Verna, Mitch'l, King/Moore, Zola^, Grant**
subs used: North/Sweeney/Proudlock · Donaldson/Eling/Westwood

3 — ROTHERHAM (H)
Town: Forecast, Stockdale, Widdowson, Bennett, Atkinson, Sweeney, Clarke, Boshell, Conlon, North", Hegarty
Rotherham: *Warrington, Tonge, Green*, Harrison, Sharps^, Fenton, Warne", Mills, Pope, Le Fondre, Law*
subs used: Proudlock/Fuller · Joseph/Cummins/Liddell

4 — BURY (A)
Town: Forecast, Stockdale, Widdowson, Leary, Atkinson, Sweeney", Clarke, Boshell, Conlon, North, Proudlock^
Bury: *Brown, Scott^, Buchanan*, Davison, Futcher, Sodje, Worrall, Bar'/Murphy, Robertson", Lowe, Jones*
subs used: Bore/Linwood/Boshell · Cresswell/Racchi/Bishop

5 — ALDERSHOT (H)
Town: Forecast, Stockdale, Widdowson, Leary^, Atkinson, Sweeney, Clarke*, Boshell, Conlon, North, Jones
Aldershot: *Jaimez-Ruiz, Blackburn, Sandell, Halls, Hinshelwood/Winfield, Harding, Morgan, Donnelly*, Soares, Hudson, Chalmers*
subs used: Linwood/Proudlock ! · Chalmers

6 — PORT VALE (A)
Town: Lillis, Stockdale, Widdowson, Leary*, Heywood, Bennett, Boshell !, Sweeney, Linwood, North, Jones
Port Vale: *Martin, Yates, McCrory, Collins, McCombe, Owen, Dodds, Loft^, Taylor", Richards*, Fraser*
subs used: Fuller · Haldane/Griffith/Richman

7 — HEREFORD (H)
Town: Lillis, Stockdale, Widdowson, Fuller, Heywood, Bennett, Clarke, Sweeney, Linwood, North, Jones
Hereford: *Bartlett, Lowe, Valentine, Rose, Jones, Lunt, Pugh, Plummer, Jackson*, Gwynne*
subs used: Clarke · Tolley/Morris

8 — TORQUAY (A)
Town: Lillis, Stockdale, Widdowson, Clarke, Atkinson, Bennett, Forbes^, Sweeney, Linwood, North", Jones
Torquay: *Poke, Robertson, Nicholson, Hargreaves, Todd^, Ellis, Stevens, Wroe, Benyon, Rendell", Williams*
subs used: Akpa Akpro/Bore/Hegarty · Thompson/Carlisle/Sills

9 — DARLINGTON (H)
Town: Lillis, Linwood, Widdowson, Clarke, Atkinson, Bennett, Forbes^, Sweeney*, Akpa Akpro^, North, Bore*
Darlington: *Hoult, Kane, Devitt, Chandler!, Miller, Foster, Smith, Bennett*, Gall, Dowsett", Main**
subs used: Forbes/Proudlock/Conlon · Main/Converty

10 — CHESTERFIELD (A)
Town: Colgan, Linwood, Widdowson, Clarke, Atkinson, Bennett, Bore, Sweeney, Proudlock, North, Forbes*
Chesterfield: *Lee, Picken, Robertson, Niven^, Page, Breckin, Lowry, Allott, Lester, McDermott/Small*, Wood*
subs used: Akpa Akpro · Gray/Bowery

11 — BARNET (A)
Town: Colgan, Linwood*, Widdowson, Clarke, Atkinson, Bennett, Bore", Sweeney, Akpa Akpro, Proudlock^, Wood
Barnet: *Cole, Devera, Gillett, Hyde M*, Yakubu, Breen, Adomah", Bolasie, Furlong, O'Flynn", Hughes*
subs used: Leary/North/Conlon · Hyde J/Jarrett/Kamdjo

Match reports

1. Conlon scrambles Town into a promising lead, but debutant Barry Hayles sets up Lee Ridley's curling equaliser. Then Hayles slides home the winner himself after good work by David Hutton. Town have plenty of the ball and go close to saving a point when Conlon drags a shot wide.

2. Calvin Zola finishes off a counter-attack with a looping shot past Forecast. Zola extends the lead with a header and immediately after the break the contest is over as Billy Jones converts a spot-kick after a push by Hegarty. Bennett hits the post, but Moore slots home the visitors' fourth.

3. Stockdale is penalised for handball and Adam Le Fondre nets from the spot. Sweeney equalises with a shot that squeezes its way past Andy Warrington. Moments later a disputed free-kick taken by Nicky Law finds Micky Cummins, whose downward header wins all three points.

4. For a second successive season, Grimsby's bad start ends at Gigg Lane. North's cross is headed home by Conlon. Loanee Forecast saves from Paul Scott and Jordan Robertson. Mike Jones gives Town trouble and Robertson misses good chances, but hard endeavour preserves the lead.

5. North has a goal disallowed before Scott Donnelly heads Gary Waddock's men ahead. Donnelly beats Forecast at the second attempt to double the lead. Conlon's late header brings Town back into it, but a late fracas sees Bennett booked and both Conlon and sub Proudlock red-carded.

6. A gloomy day all round. Louis Dodds' volley starts the rout, then Marc Richards touches in the resultant penalty. Gareth Owen heads another from a corner, Lee Collins finishing things off. challenge on Lewis Haldane, but Lillis saves the resultant penalty.

7. Town toil away in unspectacular fashion and need a rare stroke of luck to grab a late winner. North looks well offside as he seizes his chance to beat keeper Adam Bartlett at the second attempt. Newell admits: 'We are not kidding ourselves over this win, it's hard going at the moment.'

8. Gulls debutant Mark Ellis goes close with a header before Sweeney's effort has Michael Poke scrambling to save. Bore then pressurises Kevin Nicholson into slicing a clearance into his own net. Confidence soars and Sweeney strikes home a fine free-kick to clinch a very welcome win.

9. Atkinson heads Town in front. The lead lasts an hour before teenager Curtis Main nets a fine equaliser with his head. The troubled Quakers lose Jamie Chandler, red-carded for striking North in a midfield tussle. Directly after the match, the visitors sack their manager Colin Todd.

10. Derek Niven shoots in from 20 yards before ex-Mariner Jack Lester finishes off good work by Donal McDermott. The latter then adds a well-taken third goal. Proudlock immediately pulls one back with a header and then Sweeney makes it a tense finale by notching Grimsby's second.

11. A nightmare start at Underhill as John O'Flynn nets from the penalty spot and Albert Adomah swiftly makes it two. Yannick Bolasie knocks in a third goal and Town's miserable afternoon is capped by substitute Conlon being red-carded (again) in the latter stages, for violent conduct.

12 — H BURTON ALBION — 10/10

22 L 1-2 1-2 — 4,002 10 10

Jones 4 / Corbett 10, Phillips 31
Ref: S Rushton

Colgan; Krysiak, Linwood, Austin, Widdowson, Boertien, Clarke, James, Bennett, Branston, Sweeney, McGrath, Wood, Phillips, Forbes, Simpson, Jarman*, Walker^, Proudlock^, Pearson*, Jones*, Corbett
Subs: Akpa Akpro/North/Bore, Harad/Webster/Maghoma

Keeper Artur Krysiak hammers a clearance against the back of Jones and it rebounds into the net for a lucky opening goal. But Albion respond quickly, as Jimmy Phillips' cross is netted by Andy Corbett. Phillips lofts a clever finish over Colgan's head for what proves to be the winner.

13 — H ROCHDALE — 17/10

23 L 0-2 0-1 — 3,754 3 10

Rundle 24, O'Grady 85
Ref: J Moses

Colgan; Arthur, Linwood, Holmes, Widdowson, Kennedy T, Sweeney, Jones*, Bennett, McArdle, Wood, Dawson, Forbes*, Whaley, Mendy, Kennedy J, Akpa Akpro Magennis*, Dagnall, O'Grady, Rundle^, Shahin
Subs: Stephens/Thompson/Manga, Clarke/North

Adam Rundle takes a pass from Chris Dagnall, wrong-foots the home defence and puts Keith Hill's outfit ahead. Magennis hits the bar before Chris O'Grady's drive deflects out of Colgan's reach. A row behind the scenes after the game leads to the sacking of manager Mike Newell.

14 — A BOURNEMOUTH — 24/10

23 L 1-3 0-2 — 5,270 1 10

Linwood 50 / Cinnell 27, Linwood 34 (og), Pitman 87
Ref: P Gibbs

Colgan; Jalal, Linwood, Bradbury, Widdowson, Cummings, Bashell, Hollands, Lancashire Shahin*, Pearce, Sweeney, Garry, Wood, Robinson, Forbes, Molesley*, Akpa Akpro^, Connell*, Proudlock^, Feeney", Jones*, Wood
Subs: Hegarty/Magennis/Jones, Edgar/Fletcher/McQuoid

Woods takes over as caretaker, his first task to face the leaders. Alan Connell is given time to curl the first goal. Linwood deflects a cross into his own net, but later makes amends by looping a header in at the correct end. A spectacular overhead kick by Brett Pitman seals the home win.

15 — H ACCRINGTON — 30/10

23 D 2-2 1-1 — 4,325 14 11

Forbes 14, Conlon 90 / King 5, Edwards 68p
Ref: D Webb

Colgan; Dunhavin, Linwood, Winnard, Widdowson, Lees, Bashell, Procter, Lancashire I, Hegarty*, Kempson, Edwards, Bore, Joyce, Sweeney, Grant, Akpa Akpro*, Symes, Forbes^, Ryan, Proudlock^, King*
Subs: Leary/Conlon/North, McConville

Grimbarian Gary King beats Coglan at his near post. Forbes levels after Akpa Akpro's header hits the bar and falls to him. Lancashire blocks a shot with his hand and is red-carded. Phil Edwards netting the penalty. Town are rewarded when Conlon heads home with seconds remaining.

16 — A NORTHAMPTON — 14/11

23 D 0-0 0-0 — 4,028 15 12

Ref: K Stroud

Colgan; Dunn, Linwood, McCready, Widdowson, Johnson, Clarke*, Guttridge, Lancashire, Gilbert !, Atkinson I, Kanyuka, Bore, Gilligan, Sweeney, Curtis^, Forbes*, Guigan", North, Akinfenwa* Holt, Shahin^
Subs: Conlon/Widdowson/Linwood, Rodgers/Davis/McKay

Ade Akinfenwa and Liam Davis go close to breaking the deadlock either side of the break for Ian Sampson's men. Grimsby cling on to a draw, both sides ending with ten men. Debutant Peter Gilbert sees red for impeding North's path to goal, while later Town's Atkinson also departs.

17 — A LINCOLN — 21/11

23 D 0-0 0-0 — 4,981 20 13

Ref: S Tanner

Colgan; Burch, Linwood, Gordon, Widdowson" Leary, Baker, Kovacs, Lancashire Feath'stone^, Watts*, Kerr, Bore, Pulis, Sweeney, North*, Smith, Fagan", Coulson^, Clarke, Hughton
Subs: Akpa Akpro/Conlon/Shahin, Howe/Swallu

Town are cheered on by 1,200, at their lowest gate in years, and have loud penalty appeals waved away after Sweeney is upended. Loanees Coulson and Featherstone make their debuts as both sides fail to break the deadlock. Sub Rene Howe wastes a chance to win this local derby as he bursts clear but shoots wide.

18 — H BRADFORD CITY — 24/11

23 L 0-3 0-1 — 3,646 11 13

Whaley 24, Williams 60, Hanson 82
Ref: D Deadman

Colgan; Eastwood, Linwood, Ramsden, Widdowson, O'Brien L, Leary, Flynn, Lancashire, Rehman, Sweeney, Williams, Bore, Whaley, Featherstone Conlon", Bullock, Evans, Coulson^, Hanson, Shahin*, O'Brien J
Subs: Akpa Akpro/Wood/Forbes, Disley/Robinson/Bright

Neil Woods is given the manager's job on a full-time basis, but gets off to a very disappointing start. Simon Whaley's rasping drive flies past Colgan and McCrory blunders as he sets up Steve Williams with a gift for the second goal. James Hanson fires home the clincher near the end.

19 — A MACCLESFIELD — 28/11

23 D 0-0 0-0 — 1,409 19 14

Ref: K Woolmer

Colgan; Brain, Linwood, Reid, Widdowson, Tremarco, Leary, Brisley, Lancashire, Brown, Sweeney, Bencherif, Bore, Draper, Feath'stone Akpa Akpro*"Wright B^, Bell", Sinclair^, Wright*, Coulson^, Daniel
Subs: Clarke/Forbes/Proudlock, Sappleton/Tipton/Bolland

Peterborough loanee Ben Wright debuts and Town create a number of good chances. Colin Daniels' free-kick cannons off the Grimsby bar before Coulson has the same fate at the other end with a 30-yarder. Akpa Akpro misses a sitter before a late shot by sub Proudlock hits a post.

20 — H DAGENHAM & RED — 5/12

23 D 1-1 1-0 — 3,090 5 15

Coulson 36 / Nurse 60
Ref: S Bratt

Colgan; Roberts, Linwood, Day, Widdowson" Leary, Ol^Twumasi Arber, Lancashire Atkinson, Antwi*, Miller, Bore, Green, Sweeney, Currie, Feath'stone Akpa Akpro"Proudlock^ Coulson, Benson, Nurse
Subs: North/Clarke/Conlon, Doe

The recent improvement continues, but the long run without a win goes on. Featherstone's cross is collected by Coulson, who turns to thrash his shot home, ending the recent goal drought. Sweeney almost doubles the lead but hits the bar. Jon Nurse converts a cross to even things up.

21 — A SHREWSBURY — 12/12

23 D 0-0 0-0 — 4,850 10 16

Ref: A Hall

Colgan; Button, Linwood, Holden, Widdowson, McIntyre, Leary, Devitt, Lancashire* Atkinson, Coughlan, Sweeney, Langmead, Bore, Dunfield, Akpa Akpro"Proudlock^ Coulson", Leslie, Fairhurst", Elder^, Shahin*, Murray"
Subs: Featherstone/Conlon/North, Disley/Robinson/Bright

David Button is grateful to save after Proudlock slips when a good chance is created. Sub Conlon volleys narrowly over from distance and fires another chance wide. Atkinson heads in from a corner but is penalised for pushing. Paul Simpson's promotion-chasers have to settle for a draw.

22 — H MORECAMBE — 18/12

23 D 1-1 0-0 — 3,119 7 17

Sweeney 67 / Mullin 60
Ref: C Pawson

Colgan; Roche, Linwood, Parrish, Widdowson, Wilson, Leary, Artell, Lancashire Atkinson, Haining, Sweeney, Drummond, Bore, Twiss, Featherstone Akpa Akpro*"Proudlock^ Coulson, Stanley*, Mullin, Jevons^
Subs: Conlon/Jarman, Duffy/Curtis

On an icy cold Friday night, Sweeney and Coulson warm the fingers of keeper Barry Roche with fizzing drives. Against the run of play, Paul Mullin nips in to score from a corner. Deservedly, Sweeney swerves in a fine volley to clinch Grimsby's seventh draw in eight league games.

23 — H PORT VALE — 28/12

23 L 1-2 0-2 — 4,401 13 17

Conlon 90p / Rigg 7, Taylor R 41
Ref: G Sutton

Colgan; Martin, Linwood, Yates, Widdowson, Taylor, Leary, Griffith, Lancashire* Atkinson, Collins, Sweeney, Owen, Bore, Rigg, Conlon, Fraser^, Proudlock*"Coulson", Richards, Dodds, Taylor !
Subs: Widdowson/Jarman/Wright B, Lawrie

Town gift-wrap the points for Micky Adams' men. A long ball is allowed to reach Sean Rigg who shoots home under Colgan. Robert Taylor blasts the second goal, but is later red-carded for a high tackle. The resultant free-kick is handled and Conlon nets a consolation from the spot.

Match summary

No	Venue	Date	Att	Pos	Pt	Res	F-A	H-T	Scorers, Times, and Referees
24	H BURY	2/1	3,463	8	18	D	1-1	0-0	Akpa Akpro 60 / Lowe 90p — Ref: G Eltringham
25	H CHELTENHAM	16/1	3,334	22	19	D	0-0	0-0	Ref: P Tierney
26	A ROTHERHAM	23/1	3,751	4	19	L	1-2	0-2	Fletcher 90 / Le Fondre 9, 38 — Ref: E Ilderton
27	A ALDERSHOT	30/1	3,195	8	20	D	1-1	1-0	Grant 6 (og) / Hylton 68 — Ref: K Evans
28	H NOTTS COUNTY	6/2	4,452	4	20	L	0-1	0-0	Hughes 69 — Ref: M Russell
29	A BRADFORD CITY	13/2	11,321	16	21	D	0-0	0-0	Ref: S Tanner
30	A NOTTS COUNTY	17/2	5,163	6	22	D	1-1	1-1	Devitt 45 / Hughes 58 — Ref: K Wright
31	H LINCOLN	20/2	6,395	19	23	D	2-2	1-1	Peacock 38, 46 / Herd 4, Gilmour 60 — Ref: M Haywood
32	H MACCLESFIELD	23/2	4,813	20	24	D	1-1	1-0	Devitt 42 / Butcher 58 — Ref: O Langford
33	A DAGENHAM & RED	27/2	2,190	9	24	L	0-2	0-0	Scott 49, Green 86 — Ref: A Penn
34	H SHREWSBURY	6/3	3,651	7	27	W	3-0	1-0	Sinclair 45p, 57, Akpa Akpro 64 — Ref: J Moss

Squad numbers in use, subs used and reports

24 BURY (H) — Colgan, Linwood, McCrory, Leary, Atkinson, Sweeney, Featherstone, Akpa Akpro^, Proudlock*, Coulson, Bore / *(Bury)* Brown, Newey^, Buchanan, Davison*, Futcher, Sodje, Bar*, Murphy, Morrell, Lowe, Jones — subs used: Conlon/Cowan-Hall ; Scott/Racchi
A new decade, but yet another draw for Town's long-suffering fans. Proudlock backheels into Featherstone's path and he sets up Akpa Akpro to shrug off big Efe Sodje and net. Town hold on desperately until a heartbreaking last-minute penalty, given for a foul challenge by Atkinson.

25 CHELTENHAM (H) — Colgan, Linwood, McCrory, Sweeney, Atkinson, Leary, Feath'stone^, Akpa Akpro^, Proudlock*, Coulson, Bore / *(Cheltenham)* Brown, Low, Andrew, Eastham !, Gallinagh, Townsend, Labadi, Richards, Alsop, Hutton^, Pipe — subs used: Fletcher/Jarman/North ; Pook
Town dominate but unluckily have to settle for yet another draw. They find goalkeeper Scott Brown in inspired form. A penalty-kick is harshly given against Leary; Justin Richards employs a stop-start run-up, but sees his effort hit the bar. Ashley Eastham is sent off after two cautions.

26 ROTHERHAM (A) — Colgan, Linwood, McCrory, Leary, Atkinson, Sweeney, Jarman, Akpa Akpro^, Coulson, Chambers*, Bore / *(Rotherham)* Warrington, Joseph, Roberts*, Gunning, Sharps, Cummins, Law, Pope^, Le Fondre, Ellison, Mills — subs used: Proudlock/Fletcher ; Harrison/Marshall
Woods shuffles his pack, but lethal Adam le Fondre finishes off a neat early move, and then volleys home from close range following a corner. 580 Town fans have something to cheer in the near-empty Don Valley athletics stadium when sub Fletcher tucks a through ball home late on.

27 ALDERSHOT (A) — Colgan, Linwood, Widdowson, Sweeney, Atkinson, Sinclair, Proudlock*, Wright T", Peacock*, Coulson^, Bore / *(Aldershot)* Jaimez-Ruiz, Herd, Sandell, Harding, Blackburn, Charles, Bazanic, Grant^, Hylton, Soares", Jackson* — subs used: Leary/Cowan-Hall/Fletcher ; Morgan/Hylton/Hudson
An early boost as Coulson's low cross is deflected into his own net by John Grant. Sub Danny Hylton levels after the break after being put clear. A golden chance to end the winless run arrives late on as Andy Sandell handles a cross, but Proudlock scoops his spot-kick over the bar.

28 NOTTS COUNTY (H) — Colgan, Linwood, Widdowson, Sweeney, Atkinson, Sinclair, Wright T^, Fletcher*, Peacock, Coulson", Bore / *(Notts County)* Schmeichel, Thompson, Bishop, Ravenhill, Edwards, Bishop, Hughes", Hawley, Jackson, Davies, Westcar" — subs used: Jarman/Hudson/Cowan-Hall ; Clapham/Rodgers/Hamshaw
Grimsby enjoy plenty of possession but fail to create many opportunities. New forwards Tommy Wright and Lee Peacock get little joy and the pivotal moment arrives after the interval when a long kick from Kaspar Schmeichel puts Lee Hughes clear on goal and he finishes confidently.

29 BRADFORD CITY (A) — Colgan, Atkinson, Widdowson, Sweeney, Lancashire, Wright, Peacock^, Proudlock*, Coulson*, Sinclair, Bore / *(Bradford City)* Glennon, Ramsden, O'Brien L, Flynn, Rehman, Williams, Evans*, Hanson, Thorne", Bullock, Neilson" — subs used: Akpa Akpro/Leary/Hudson ; Boulding/Osborne/Brandon
The managerless Bantams press hard but find Colgan in good form for Grimsby. Sweeney goes close with a 20-yarder that Matt Glennon tips around a post. Ex-Mariner Michael Boulding just misses, as does Lee Bullock, but Town hold firm. It's now 21 league games without a win.

30 NOTTS COUNTY (A) — Colgan, Atkinson, Widdowson, Sweeney, Lancashire, Devitt, Wright T^, Proudlock*, Hudson, Sinclair*, Bore / *(Notts County)* Schmeichel, Thompson, Bishop, Ravenhill, Edwards, Bishop*, Hughes /, Hawley, Rodgers, Davies, Clapham — subs used: Leary/Akpa Akpro/Fletcher ; Westcar/Hamshaw
Lee Hughes nods in his 23rd of the season from Ben Davies' cross. County almost double the lead when Davies' effort forces an unorthodox save from Colgan. Moments before the interval, Widdowson's cross finds debutant Jamie Devitt who curls a fine shot into the top left corner.

31 LINCOLN (H) — Colgan, Atkinson, Widdowson, Devitt, Lancashire, Sinclair, Wright T*, Peacock, Hudson, Coulson, Bore / *(Lincoln)* Burch, Pearce, Anderson, Watts*, Kerr, Lennon, Gilmour^, Broughton, Saunders, Hughton, Herd — subs used: Fletcher ; Swaibu/John-Lewis
Ben Herd pokes in Drewe Broughton's headed pass. Peacock levels from a Devitt free-kick. Coulson goes on a run and his cross is buried at the second attempt by Peacock. A disputed penalty from Brian Gilmour is saved, but he nets the rebound. Officials miss a late Herd handball.

32 MACCLESFIELD (H) — Colgan, Atkinson, Widdowson, Devitt*, Lancashire, Leary*, Wright T^, Peacock, Hudson, Coulson", Bore / *(Macclesfield)* Brain, Reid, Brisley, Bell, Brown, Hessey, Wright*, Sappleton, Draper, Daniel, Butcher — subs used: Akpa Akpro/Jarman I/Proud'k ; Tipton
Recalled Leary goes off with a head injury. Tommy Wright misses a good chance before Akpa Akpro's finds Devitt, who nets a well-taken goal. Richard Butcher curls in a free-kick which deceives Colgan. Jarman is sent off after a scuffle. Town have now drawn 14 of their last 18.

33 DAGENHAM & RED (A) — Oxley, Atkinson, Widdowson, Devitt*, Lancashire, Sweeney", Wright T*, Peacock, Hudson, Sinclair, Bore / *(Dagenham & Red)* Roberts, Ogogo, McCrory, Arber, Doe, Pack, Montgom'y*, Benson, Scott^, Gain, Green" — subs used: Akpa Akpro/Proud'k/Coulson ; Folly/Nurse/Thomas
John Still's Daggers are well on top for the first half but cannot break through until Josh Scott stoops to head in after the break. Danny Green fires into the corner past debutant Mark Oxley to seal the points. Town's horrendous run goes on — it's now 25 league games without a victory.

34 SHREWSBURY (H) — Colgan, Atkinson*, Widdowson, Sweeney, Lancashire, Devitt^, Sinclair, Akpa Akpro", Peacock, Coulson, Bore / *(Shrewsbury)* Button, Murray, Skarz, Neal, Coughlan, Langmead, Hibbert, Cureton^, Leslie, McIntyre, Dunfield* — subs used: Linwood/Hegarty/Proudlock ; Robinson/Van den Broek
Tactical changes pay off at last. Akpa Akpro is bundled over and Sinclair nets from the penalty spot. Sinclair is on hand to grab a second goal after Akpa Akpro has two efforts blocked. Major celebrations for Grimsby fans as Akpa Akpro ensures victory with a superb left-foot volley.

35 A CREWE 9/3 · 3,272 · 23 · L · 2.4 · 15 · 27
Akpa Akpro 32, Sinclair 41
Moore 29, Grant 35, West'd 55, Don'n 90
Ref: C Webster

Colgan	Linwood	Widdowson	Sweeney^	Atkinson	Devitt*	Bore	Sinclair	Akpa Akpro	Peacock	Coulson"	Hegarty/Leary/Produlock
Phillips	Brayford	Tootle*	Bailey	O'Donnell	Mitchel/King Westwood	Donaldson	Moore	Miller	Grant'	Martin !/Schumacher	

Bryan Moore shoots home from 12 yards before Akpa Akpro finds the corner of the net. Joel Grant restores the lead but Sinclair swoops to level once again. Ashley Westwood and Clayton Donaldson net stunning goals either side of sub Carl Martin being red-carded for a bad tackle.

---

36 A MORECAMBE 13/3 · 1,882 · 23 · D · 1-1 · 13 · 28
Coulson 59
Mullin 41
Ref: D Webb

Colgan	Linwood	Widdowson	Leary	Atkinson	Hegarty^	Bore	Wright	Akpa Akpro	Peacock*	Coulson	Hudson/Proudlock
Roche	Parrish	Wilson	Bentley	Haining	Drummond	Hackney"	Panther"	Mullin	Jevons*	Duffy	Curtis/Wainwright/Stanley

Injury-hit Grimsby hold Sammy McIlory's lads at bay until Paul Mullins heads home at the far post. Akpa Akpro scoops a great chance over before Mullin hits the Town bar. Coulson levels from Widdowson's pass against the run of play. The club now sits six points adrift of safety.

---

37 H BOURNEMOUTH 20/3 · 4,428 · 23 · W · 3-2 · 3 · 31
Devitt 27, Coulson 61, Chambers 90
Bradbury 42, Feeney 62
Ref: R Shoebridge

Colgan	Atkinson	Widdowson	Devitt*	Sweeney	Bore	Sinclair	Akpa Akpro	Peacock	Coulson"	Chambers/Hudson
Jalal	Bradbury	Wiggins	Hollands	Garry	Bartley	Hollands*	Robinson	Pitman"	Fletcher	Feeney	McQuoid"/Partton/Goulding !

Devitt slams home Town's first, but unmarked Lee Bradbury levels. Coulson nets from a corner but Liam Feeney's shot slides under Colgan. Sub Jeff Goulding is sent off for elbowing debutant Jude Stirling. Sub Chambers nets Coulson's cross in a thrilling climax. Another win.

---

38 H ROCHDALE 27/3 · 4,724 · 23 · L · 1-4 · 1 · 31
Chambers 43
Thompson 17, Dagnall 20, 41, 90
Ref: F Graham

Colgan	Atkinson	Widdowson	Sweeney	Stirling*	Sinclair*	Bore	Chambers^	Akpa Akpro	Peacock	Hudson/Proudlock/Lancashire
Fielding	Wiseman	Kennedy T	Toner	Stanton	McArdle	Jones	Kennedy J	Dagnall	O'Grady^	Thompson	Higginbotham

Ex-Mariner Ciaran Toner crosses for Joe Thompson to head the first. Chris Dagnall pounces on a loose ball for the second goal and is then set up by Chris O'Grady for 3-0. Chambers pulls one back for Grimsby before Dagnall strokes the ball past Colgan to complete a smart hat-trick.

---

39 H NORTHAMPTON 2/4 · 6,482 · 23 · L · 1-2 · 8 · 31
Coulson 42
Davis 18, Akinfenwa 68
Ref: A Taylor

Oxley	Atkinson	Widdowson	Sweeney	Lancashire !	Leary	Bore	Devitt*	Akpa Akpro	Peacock	Coulson^	Heywood/Forbes
Steel	Gilbert	Johnson	Guttridge	Hinton	Beckwith	Gilligan	Osman	McKay*	Akinfenwa	Davis^	Guinan/Dyer

A bumper Good Friday crowd is subdued as the Cobblers net in their first attack. Ade Akinfenwa setting up Liam Davis. Coulson turns and fires a fine equaliser. Lancashire is sent off for alleged use of the elbow. Akinfenwa swoops for a winner, nodding in Luke Guttridge's cross.

---

40 A ACCRINGTON 5/4 · 1,839 · 23 · W · 3-2 · 14 · 34
Hudson 56, Coulson 58, Devitt 61
Kee 38, Symes 44
Ref: S Rushton

Oxley	Atkinson	Widdowson	Devitt	Lancashire	Sinclair*	Bore	Hudson	Akpa Akpro	Wright T*	Coulson^	Leary/Sweeney/Proudlock
Bouzanis	Winnard	McCarten	Procter	Kempson	Edwards	Turner^	Ryan"	Symes	Kee'	Grant	Joyce/McConville/Miles

Town dominate early on but succumb to a Billy Kee header and a Michael Symes curler. A sensational comeback sees Town score three in five minutes – Hudson's header, Coulson's deflected free-kick and Devitt's superb curling shot. Survival is still unlikely, but this gives some hope.

---

41 A HEREFORD 10/4 · 2,143 · 23 · W · 1-0 · 16 · 37
Devitt 18
Ref: N Miller

Colgan	Atkinson	Widdowson	Devitt	Lancashire	Sinclair	Bore	Hudson	Akpa Akpro	Wright T*	Coulson"	Stirling
Bartlett	Green	Valentine	Rose	Jones	Lunt	Pugh	Young*	Manset	Jarvis^	McQuilkin	Done/McCallum

Town are definitely up for the fight and Wright goes close in the first minute. Wright lays the ball off to Devitt who scores with a trademark curling drive. Adam Bartlett tips a Sinclair rocket on to his post. Darren Jones goes close to a last-gasp equaliser that would have been unjust.

---

42 H CHESTERFIELD 13/4 · 5,648 · 23 · D · 2.2 · 6 · 38
Wright T 28, Akpa Akpro 57
Lester 65, 75
Ref: K Wright

Colgan	Atkinson	Widdowson	Devitt	Sinclair	Bore	Hudson	Akpa Akpro	Wright T*	Coulson	Peacock
Lee	Whing	Goodall	Niven"	Page	Breckin	Demont'gnac.Allott	Lester	Boden^	Bowery	Boshell/Gritton

Wright outpaces defenders to net his first Grimsby goal. Akpa Akpro shrugs off a challenge to fire high into the net. What seems a certain win is snatched away as ex-Town hero Jack Lester shows his finishing skills twice in ten minutes. Eager appeals for a late Town penalty are denied.

---

43 H TORQUAY 17/4 · 5,702 · 23 · L · 0-3 · 19 · 38
Wroe 54p, Benyon 62, Carayol 71
Ref: G Salisbury

Colgan	Atkinson	Widdowson	Devitt	Sinclair*	Bore	Hudson	Akpa Akpro	Wright T^	Coulson	Sweeney/Peacock
Poke	Mansell	Nicholson	Ellis	Branston !	Robertson	Carayol^	Wroe	Benyon*	Rendel"	Zebroski	Charnock/Thompson/O'Kane

Elliott Benyon is brought down by Lancashire, and Nicky Wroe nets from the spot. A bad day for Town is capped by Benyon's bullet into the top corner, and a close-range effort from Mustapha Carayol. Guy Branston departs after two cautions. The victory ensures the Gulls' survival.

---

44 H DARLINGTON 24/4 · 1,911 · 23 · W · 2-0 · 24 · 41
Lancashire 20, Akpa Akpro 45
Ref: M Haywood

Colgan	Atkinson	Widdowson	Devitt*	Lancashire	Sinclair*	Bore	Hudson	Akpa Akpro*	Peacock	North/Linwood/Wright T
Liversedge	Giddings"	Milne	Dempsey	White	Bower	Smith	Groves*	Purcell	Diop	Mulligan^	McReady/Convery/Madden

A tiny crowd assembles in already-doomed Darlington's huge new stadium. They see Grimsby's slim survival hopes kept alive as Lancashire heads in Sweeney's corner. Akpa Akpro doubles the lead just before the break, a neat side-footed shot beating Nick Liversedge from ten yards.

---

45 H BARNET 1/5 · 7,033 · 23 · W · 2-0 · 22 · 44
Atkinson 59, Hudson 90
Ref: N Miller

Colgan	Atkinson	Widdowson	Devitt	Lancashire	Sinclair^	Bore	Hudson	Akpa Akpro	Wright T*	Coulson^	Peacock/Leary/Forbes
Cole	Deen	Gillett	Hyde M^	Devera	Breen	Adomah	Jarrett*	Furlong	O'Flynn"	Hughes	James/Deverdics/Vilhete

A victory today will ensure the fight goes into the final day. Relegation rivals Barnet this week sacked manager Ian Hendon. In a tense, raucous atmosphere, defender Atkinson swivels and cracks home a beauty. Deep into stoppage time Hudson strides clear and drives home the clincher.

---

46 A BURTON 8/5 · 5,510 · 23 · L · 0-3 · 13 · 44
Pearson 10, Harrad 37, 58
Ref: A Bates

Colgan	Atkinson	Widdowson	Devitt*	Sinclair*	Bore	Hudson	Akpa Akpro	Peacock	Coulson	Sweeney/Chambers
Poole	Taylor	Boertien	James	Parkes	McGrath	Baco	Penn"	Pearson	Harrad	Simpson	Webster

Town must win to stay up and hope Barnet don't beat Rochdale. It all goes pear-shaped when Akpa Akpro hits a post and Burton break to the other end for Greg Pearson to net. Shaun Harrad's double strike seals Grimsby's fate. A minority of the noisy 2,100 away fans cause trouble.

Average 3,272 · Home Average 4,458 · Away 3,794

Carling (League) Cup

		Att	F-A	H-T	Scorers, Times, and Referees	SQUAD NUMBERS IN USE											subs used
1 A TRANMERE	11/8	3,527	L 0-4	0-3	[Curran 40, Edds 71] McLaren 32, Thomas-Moore 37p. Ref: A Taylor	Colgan *Daniels*	Stockdale *Logan*	Widdowson *Cresswell*	Hegarty *McLaren"*	Bennett *Broomes*	Atkinson *Goodison^*	Sweeney^ *Shuker*	Boshell *Welsh*	Akpa Akpro *Tho'-Moore***	Conlon *Curran*	Proudlock* *Mahon*	North/Leary Garnell/Edds/Taylor

John Barnes' first home game in charge of Rovers sees them win comfortably despite conceding much of the possession. Paul McLaren nods home a rebound, and Ian Thomas-Moore converts a penalty. Unmarked Craig Curran converts a deep cross and Gareth Edds heads in a corner.

FA Cup

		Att	F-A	H-T	Scorers, Times, and Referees	SQUAD NUMBERS IN USE											subs used
1 H BATH CITY	7/11	2,103 NL	L 0-2	0-1	Holland 32, Edwards 52 Ref: P Quinn	Colgan *Robinson*	Wood *Jombati*	Widdowson" *Rollo*	Leary *Jones*	Linwood *Holland*	Atkinson *Connolly*	Bore^ *Simpson*	Boshell *Badman*	Akpa Akpro* *Edwards***	Conlon *Mohamed^*	Shahin *Hogg*	North/Jones/Fuller Douglas/Perrott

Conlon misses with an early header and Town go on to suffer a humiliating cup exit. City skipper Chris Holland plants a firm header beyond Colgan. Sub North goes close before Darren Edwards nets a curling shot from 20 yards. After years of misery this represents a new low point.

Johnstone's Paint (FL) Tr

		Att	F-A	H-T	Scorers, Times, and Referees	SQUAD NUMBERS IN USE											subs used
N2 A HARTLEPOOL	6/10	1,675 1:15	W 2-0	2-0	Sweeney 6, Proudlock 34 Ref: N Miller	Colgan *Flinders*	Fuller" *Austin*	Widdowson *Haslam*	Bennett *McSweeney^Collins*	Wood *Monkhouse*	Atkinson *Liddle*	Sweeney *Rowell*	Jarman^ *Larkin*	Boshell ! *Bjornsson***	Forbes *Humphreys*	Proudlock* *Behan/Boyd*	Leary/Clarke/Akpa Akpro

After getting a bye in the northern section first round, Town shock the League One club formerly managed by Mike Newell, Sweeney curling in a superb early free-kick. Bennett then sets up Proudlock who clips in a neat goal. Boshell is red-carded after pulling back sub Denis Behan.

		Att	F-A	H-T	Scorers, Times, and Referees	SQUAD NUMBERS IN USE											subs used
N A LEEDS QF	10/11	10,430 1:1	L 1:3	0:2	Sweeney 57, [Beckford 55] Lancashire 40 (og), Kilkenny 45, Ref: A Penn	Colgan *Ankergran*	Bore *White*	McCrory *Hughes*	Leary *Kilkenny*	Lancashire *Michalik*	Atkinson *Naylor*	Sweeney *Gradel*	Clarke" *Snodgrass**Beckford*	North^ *Vokes^*	Forbes* *Johnson"*	Shahin *Conlon/Akpa Akpro/Wood*	Robinson/Showunmi/Prutton

In front of a live TV audience, Town collapse to three goals in 15 minutes. Max Gradel's low cross is diverted in by Lancashire. Neil Kilkenny picks his spot with a 20-yarder, then Jermaine Beckford shows neat footwork to grab a third. A spectacular volley by Sweeney claws one back.

League table

	P	W	D	L	F	A	W	D	L	F	A	Pts
		Home					Away					
1 Notts County	46	16	6	1	58	14	11	6	6	38	17	93
2 Bournemouth	46	16	3	4	33	16	9	5	9	28	28	83
3 Rochdale	46	14	3	6	45	20	11	4	8	37	28	82
4 Morecambe	46	14	6	3	44	24	6	7	10	29	40	73
5 Rotherham	46	10	9	4	29	18	11	1	11	26	34	73
6 Aldershot	46	12	7	4	43	24	8	5	10	26	32	72
7 Dag.&Red*	46	15	2	6	46	27	5	10	8	23	31	72
8 Chesterfield	46	14	3	6	38	27	7	4	12	23	35	70
9 Bury	46	11	6	6	29	23	8	6	9	25	36	69
10 Port Vale	46	8	8	7	32	25	9	5	9	29	25	68
11 Northampton	46	9	9	5	29	21	9	4	10	33	32	67
12 Shrewsbury	46	10	6	7	30	20	7	6	10	25	34	63
13 Burton	46	9	5	9	38	34	8	6	9	31	37	62
14 Bradford C	46	8	8	7	28	27	8	6	9	31	35	62
15 Accrington	46	11	1	11	38	39	7	6	10	24	35	61
16 Hereford	46	12	4	7	32	25	5	4	14	22	40	59
17 Torquay	46	9	5	9	34	24	5	9	9	30	31	57
18 Crewe	46	7	4	12	35	36	8	6	9	33	37	55
19 Macclesfield	46	7	8	8	27	28	5	10	8	22	30	54
20 Lincoln	46	9	7	7	25	26	4	4	15	17	39	50
21 Barnet	46	8	10	5	30	18	4	2	17	17	45	48
22 Cheltenham	46	5	8	10	34	38	5	10	8	20	33	48
23 GRIMSBY	46	4	9	10	25	36	5	8	10	20	35	44
24 Darlington	46	3	3	17	14	40	5	3	15	19	47	30
	1104	241	141	170	816	630	170	141	241	630	816	1515

* promoted
after play-offs

Odds & ends

Double wins: (1) Hereford.
Double losses: (5) Crewe, Rotherham, Burton, Rochdale, Port Vale.

Won from behind: (1) Accrington (a).
Lost from in front: (2) Cheltenham (h), Burton (h).

High spots: The late-season fight-back after all had seemed lost.
Victory at Accrington, from 0-2 down at half-time.
Victory in the tense final home match, to set up a dramatic last day.
Good away support, even on the longest trips.
Ashley Chambers' dramatic winner in March, to end the barren spell.

Low spots: Relegation out of the Football League after 99 years.
The mid-season sequence of 25 games without victory.
The sacking of Mike Newell and subsequent fall-out.
Unsettled squad: 42 different players used in 50 games (24 debutants).
The pitch invasions and associated trouble on the final day at Burton.
The humiliating FA Cup exit at the hands of little Bath City.

Player of the Year: Peter Bore.
Top scorer: (6) Peter Sweeney.
Ever-presents: (0).
Hat-tricks for: (0).
Hat-tricks against: (1) Chris Dagnall (Rochdale) (a).

Appearances and Goals

	Appearances								Goals				
	Lge	Sub	LC	Sub	FAC	Sub	JPT	Sub	Lge	Sub	LCFAC	JPT	Tt
Akpa Akpro, Jean-Lou'	26	10					1	2	5				5
Atkinson, Robert	37		1		1		1		2				2
Bennett, Ryan	13				1		1						
Bore, Peter	37	3			1		1		2				2
Boshell, Danny	5	1	1				1						
Chambers, Ashley	2	2					1		2				2
Clarke, Jamie	9	4						1					
Colgan, Nick	35		1		1								
Conlon, Barry	7	9			1		1		5				5
Coulson, Michael	28	7							5				5
Cowan-Hall, Paris		3											
Devitt, Jamie	15								5				5
Featherstone, Nicky	7	1					1		1				1
Fletcher, Wes	1	5											
Forbes, Adrian	8	5				2			1				1
Forecast, Tommy	4												
Fuller, Josh	2	3			1		1						
Heywood, Matt	1												
Hegarty, Nick	5	4						1					
Hudson, , Mark	11	5							2				2
Jarman, Nathan	2	5											
Jones, Chris	6	1						1					
Lancashire, Olly	24	1	1		1								
Leary, Michael	19	9			1	1	1	1	1				1
Lillis, Josh	4												
Linwood, Paul	23	5	1		1		1		1				1
Magennis, Josh	1	1											
McCrory, Damien	10						1						
Mendy, Arnaud	1												
North, Danny	9	8	1		1		1		1				1
Oxley, Mark	3												
Peacock, Lee	14	3					1		2				2
Proudlock, Adam	14	13	1		1		1		1			1	2
Shahin, Jammal	4	1			1								
Sinclair, Dean	16								3				3
Stirling, Jude	2	2											
Stockdale, Robbie	8	1											
Sweeney, Peter	36	4			1		2	1	4			2	6
Widdowson, Joe	36	2	1		1		1						
Wood, Bradley	7	1			1		1						
Wright, Ben	1												
Wright, Tommy	13	1					1		2				2
42 players used	506	114	11	2	11	3	22	6	45			3	48

LEAGUE TWO (The final match)   Grimsby fans in full voice at Burton Albion   SEASON 2009-10

Printed in Great Britain
by Amazon

11899111R00093